COUNTRY IN MY HEART

*Success stories of people
who prayed for a country home*

COMPILED AND EDITED
BY JERE AND LINDA FRANKLIN

Country In My Heart
Copyright © 2014 by Jere and Linda Franklin
A Rainbow Heart Publication

Reproduction of the stories in this book are unrestricted.
Printed by Review and Herald Graphics, Published by Rainbow Heart Productions.
Cover and Interior Design: Madelyn Ruiz
Typeset: Adobe Garamond Pro 12/18
This book was also edited by Ruth Maddy

Other writings by Jere Franklin:

Books: *God's Appointed*; story of Christian courtship principles in action

You Can Survive! (English/Spanish); a survival and revival tool for end time preparation

Pamphlets: *At the Border of Canaan:* Where Ancient Israel failed, victory is necessary!

Conspiracy Theory: Does Satan have a plot that God cannot overrule?

Order of Service: Each element of the liturgy is significant.

Ribbon of Blue: Today's outward symbol of loyalty to God

Tithe: Does God say where the tenth of our income should go?

True Education for the End Times: Critical building blocks that everyone should know

God's Last Effort: God wants to awaken His people, by A. M. Dart (reprinted with permission)

Chart (24- by 36-inches): Closing Events Chart in English and Spanish

Other books by Linda Franklin:

Rainbow in the Flames; healing journey and love story of Jed Franklin, burn survivor

On a Wing and a Prayer series (books 1-3); uplifting, incredible encounters with birds

Order books, pamphlets, and charts: www.youcansurvive.org, ruth@youcansurvive.org,
or Ruth Maddy 509-369-2671

Library and Archives Canada Cataloguing in Publication

Country in my heart : success stories of people who prayed
for a country home / compiled and   edited by Jere and Linda Franklin.

Includes index.
ISBN 978-0-9688901-7-2   (pbk.)

1. Country life--Religious aspects--Christianity. 2. Country life--
United States. 3. Country life--Canada. 4. Christian biography.
I. Franklin, Jere C. (Jere Calvin), 1939-, editor II. Franklin, Linda L. (Linda Loretta), 1947- editor

BV4501.3.C68 2014   248.4'86732   C2014-902468-1

Dedication

This book is dedicated to Kenya
(our precious gift-daughter)
whose escape from the city is absolutely inspiring,
who believes in country living
more than anyone else we know,
and from whom we continue to learn
lessons of God's restorative power.
(Kenya's story is chapter 11).

In Appreciation

A big thanks to all of those who
took time to record and send us
their amazing and uplifting stories of
God's providences
in their discovery of a country home.

COUNTRY IN MY HEART

Success stories of people
who prayed for a country home

Table of Contents

Introduction

The stories in *Country In My Heart* were sent to us by friends who have received tangible answers to prayer when they seriously sought a home in the country. Think of these stories as a country buffet! Like a specialty dish, each story comes directly from the hand of an individual who has tasted success and is passing the recipe on to a friend. The manuscripts are essentially unchanged, save for our introductory remarks. Most of these folks have attended at least one of our *You Can Survive!* (*YCS*) seminars, and some of them moved to the country as a result of attending that series. In each case, serious obstacles stood in the way of their country dream, but these are real people with real names and they have each had a truly "moving experience". Our God is a prayer-answering God!

We have shared our country living seminars in the United States, Canada, Europe, and Africa. We have heard many encouraging stories, but we've heard a few good excuses, too:

"Maybe later."

"This is home."

"I can't find work."

"Too inconvenient."

"I'm too far in debt."

"Don't like gardening."

"My kids are in school."

"Much too big a change."

"I don't like getting dirty."
"It's too far from the mall."
"I'm afraid of wild animals."
"I can't empty a mouse trap."
"I can't find the right property."
"I'm trapped by circumstances."
"I have to care for my aged parents."
"I already tried it and it doesn't work for me."
"I've never even heard about country living until this weekend!"

If you can read yourself into one of these challenges, take heart! God can not only find a way for you to move to the country, He will even change the desires of your heart, if you allow Him. Dare to begin this journey of faith! Make your best effort! The old hymn tells the truth, "God will take care of you!"

The other day someone told us, "Funny how 'getting away from it all' can lead you to discover everything you've been missing!" We strongly believe that moving to the country, with the spirit of truly leaving the city and its artificialities and allurements, will be the means of developing the return to innocence that God is looking for in His remnant people. It will develop the "hearing ear" and the "seeing eye". God's guidance is available. Nothing, in the life of a Christian, is a coincidence.

The writers of these stories are saying: "If it can happen for me, it can happen for you!" These writers overcame great obstacles; financial challenges, interference, temporary housing, and being classified as fanatical. Heaven was on their side when they decided to move out.

There is not one family in a hundred who will be improved physically, men-

tally, or spiritually by residing in the city. Faith, hope, love, happiness, can far better be gained in retired places, where there are fields and hills and trees. Take your children away from the sights and sounds of the city… and their minds will become more healthy. It will be found easier to bring home to their hearts the truth of the word of God (*The Adventist Home*, page 137).

Enthusiastic Testimonials

"I know that the time of the end is approaching because of the increase in natural disasters, and other prophetic indicators. I want to be ready for the end."

"I knew that God must have a plan for His people, but I was unclear as to how to discern or implement that plan. Now I have a starting platform."

"I have never heard that country living was God's plan for His people, but I see it now. Why didn't I realize it before? …before I was so far in debt? …before it became so difficult to cut my connections? …before my children were grown and gone?"

Provision and Protection

Sanctuary Ranch (chapter eight) was God's gift to us. Twice ours, it is not just a home in the country, it is our heritage. In spite of having never seen our ranch before we bought it, we had conclusive evidences that God was leading us to purchase it. Subsequently, there have been enough significant providences over the past forty years that, in spite of nearly overpowering discouragements, He has been able to assure us of His guidance. Quite recently, in fact, He sent me an "updated memo".

It was about a month before our 2010 Family Camp when I (Linda) went out to the garden early one morning to pick some raspberries for breakfast. On the way to the garden, I noticed some grasshoppers. We'd been hearing horror stories about the local plague from customers who had bought bedding plants from us. These bold insects were stripping plants from gardens, patio pots, and even cleaning out window boxes! I had considered those stories to be an exaggeration, but I suddenly sensed that we were in deep trouble. In four short weeks, we had committed to provide the noon meal for our Family Camp guests from this very garden! My heart went out to God in a plea for protection.

Several days later, fully expecting to see some serious damage, there was still no evidence of invasion. Even our colorful rainbow chard had no holes in the leaves!

"It's a miracle!" I breathed as I stood, once again, in the middle of our garden the last week before Family Camp. Still no grasshopper damage! That's when I noticed the robins busily running through our rows of lettuce, green beans, and cabbage. Lots and lots of robins! It seemed that several relatives must have joined our usual Ranch House flock. I tried counting the birds, but they wouldn't hold still, but I was pretty sure that there was more than twenty birds. Why so many? What were they doing? You guessed it—eating grasshoppers!

We had knelt together and surrendered our garden to God at the beginning of the growing season; now I understood that this orchestration of protection was a foretaste of how God's remnant will survive earth's last, unrelenting storm. By surrendering all that we have, and all that we are, He will bless our land (2 Chronicles 7:14) so that we will have food to eat and to share. Yes, He can still "rebuke the devourer" (Malachi 3:11). I saw it myself!

No More Doubts

Country In My Heart stories will help remove any lingering doubts you might have about God's willingness to help His people. These stories are from people who had little hope of finding a home in the country and they give God total credit! There *is* a special place that God has prepared for you, too! Believe it!

Not more surely is the place prepared for us in the heavenly mansions than is the special place designated on earth where we are to work for God (*Christ's Object Lessons*, pp. 326-327).

It is our hope that the stories collected in this first volume of *Country In My Heart* will encourage you to trust that He is able and willing to lead you to your country home.

We have nothing to fear for the future, except as we shall forget the way the Lord has led us, and His teaching in our past history (*Selected Messages*, book 3, page 162).

CODA

We welcome your story about how God answers your prayers for a country home. Send your story to us, a Word document via e-mail.

Jere and Linda Franklin
P.O. Box 840
Chetwynd, BC V0C 1J0
www.youcansurvive.org

Invitation to Country Living

LINDA FRANKLIN

*A return to simpler methods will be appreciated by children
and youth... Study in agricultural lines should be the
A, B, and C of the education given in our schools.
This is the very first work that should be entered upon
(Testimonies for the Church, vol. 4, p. 179).*

Country Home—Preference or Principle?

"The recession is inspiring more young families and singles to head out
of the city and back to the country," claims the December 2, 2009 article
in The Wall Street Journal entitled, "Green Acres is the Place to Be."

"Motivations can vary, but typically there are three groups: young people buying land as an asset or investment with vague hopes of living on it someday; exurban commuters who have jobs in big towns or cities but want to escape the sprawl; and back-to-the-land types who dabble in hobby farming."

One man who was interviewed for the article said, "Fear sometimes is a good thing and will push you to do things you ordinarily wouldn't." The following comments were posted in response to the article:

1) "My kids love it out here," said a single mother of four who works 40 hours a week outside the home. "This lifestyle is not for sissies, it is hard work and takes dedication and courage." Some days, when she was overtired, she'd tell the children, "I quit! We are moving back to the city! Then something tells me to keep going. That something was usually my children. They are amazing… I know I made the right decision to live this way… I am staying where I am and will never think about giving up again."

2) "Common sense, isn't that the point? We have reached a point in our society where everyone needs to find some means of self-preservation."

3) "I grew up in the country and it's the best life there is. There's nothing like it. We grow a lot of what we eat… have the satisfaction of knowing what is in our food. We do a lot of organic gardening. I would not exchange farm life for anything. We sell produce… and make enough money to pay our yearly taxes… it's a really fun way to live."

Urban Stress

Reasons for moving to the country may not include a spiritual thrust, but many people in the US and Canada have recently sold their city homes and relocated in the country because they know it is best for their own health, their children's upbringing, and peace of mind with regard to the economic future.

CBC News online posted (June 22, 2011) a study by Jens Pruessner, of McGill University, that revealed changes in the structure of the brain due to urban stress. His findings conclude that the strain of dealing with population density, traffic, type of housing, and other anxieties of city living increase the risk of depression and anxiety. Schizophrenia rates are much higher in people born in and brought up in the cities. The study, funded by the European Community's Seventh Framework Program, The German Research Foundation, and the Federal Ministry of Education and Research in Germany, revealed, through MRI scans of brain responses, increased activity in two areas of the brain known to process emotions.

"Our results identify distinct neural mechanisms for an established environmental risk factor," says Pruessner, "and link the urban environment for the first time to social stress processing, and suggest that brain regions differ in vulnerability to this risk factor across the lifespan. The findings contribute to our understanding of environmental risk for mental disorders and health in general."

The Christian Invitation

Repeated studies on stress reveal that a quiet environment is more conducive to mental and physical health. This holds true for spiritual growth as well. The Lord says, in Psalm 46:10, "Be still and know that I am God." What better education is there than this knowledge? To know His will, personally, is worth every effort it might take to achieve that quietness. It can be found.

In "Heeding the Clarion Call" (*Visitor*, February 2012), Sean Belony interviewed Buddy and Beth Ackman. His introduction captures the essence of God's invitation to country living:

> Evidences of approaching end-time events have been the topic of conversation among Seventh-day Adventists for more than a century. We preach that God's word points in brilliant clarity to his soon return, like billboards for our journey. Yet, to many, His second coming has never felt more imminent. Wars and rumors of wars. Civil unrest. Global economic uncertainty. A multiplication of natural disasters the world over. Not unlike the clear shrills of a trumpet, God's people of our generation feel beckoned to revival!

> Some, like Buddy and Beth Ackman, argue that Earth's "birth pangs" are calling us to action, "to get out of the cities as fast as possible" as Ellen White instructs in *Testimonies for the Church* (vol. 6, p. 195). In their effort to prepare for our heavenly home with Christ, the Ackmans made a difficult decision to leave behind their bustling life in a Washington D. C. suburb. They have taken up residence in rural West Virginia… and hope their transition to simpler living will inspire other Adventists to consider making "the move".

According to the interview, the Ackmans learned about the call to country living by attending an "Out of the Cities" meeting by Dave Westbrook. Testing the Lord's leading, Buddy put his mechanic business up for sale. It was gone in 6 weeks! They put their house up for sale. The first people who looked at the house bought it! Then the housing market crashed. In a very organized search pattern, they found where they wanted to locate and Buddy again started a business.

Buddy says, "It's not something we just jumped into in a day. We took our time… It's something we felt we should have done a long time ago… I wanted to make sure it was the right time. I believe when you have children, it's good to follow this counsel." He adds, "We were glad to give up TV!"

Beth says of the move, "We tried to downsize, leaving behind books, clothing and furniture." Her advice to those who are considering a move to the country, "Pray, pray, pray! …you need to understand why you are doing this. It's not something you're going to be able to do in the time of trouble. There is so much involved. You have to get a house established, start a garden…get tools…help your children in their spiritual walk…attend seminars."

Both Buddy and Beth feel certain that they are where the Lord would have them to be located.

Bible Times and Today

There is no question about the advantages of being able to grow food, especially with economic pressures on the horizon.

In his Proverbs, King Solomon advised his people to give agriculture a high priority: 12:11—*He that tilleth his land shall be satisfied with bread; and 24:27—Prepare thy work without, and make it fit for thyself in the field; and afterwards build thine house.*

There is always a bigger picture than we can see. God's infinite vision includes the future. With divine enlightenment, we might catch a glimpse of the overwhelming possibilities and be prepared. Country living is a special invitation by which God is expressing His love to us, warning us not to be found living where He will begin cleansing the earth.

There are reasons why we should not build in the cities. On these cities, God's judgments are soon to fall. …The time is near when large cities will be swept away, and all should be warned of these coming judgments (Country Living, p. 8).

The work of the people of God is to prepare for the events of the future, which will soon come upon them with blinding force (Country Living, p. 10).

From God's point of view, considering His revelation of what is coming upon the world, what wiser choice could we make than to live in the country?

Buy or Sell?

There is advice is the Spirit of Prophecy with regard to the buying and selling of property. Sometimes it says "sell", sometimes "buy". Some might find it confusing, but it's not meant to be; properties that will be of no use in the time of trouble (investments, places where we cannot grow food, do not have our own well, no wood, etc.) must be sold, and country properties purchased and adapted to farming (agricultural land, trees, water, good air, elbow room, etc.).

I was shown that it is the will of God that the saints should cut loose from every encumbrance before the time of trouble comes, and make a covenant with God through sacrifice. If they have their property on the altar and earnestly inquire of God for duty, He will teach them when to dispose of these things. Then they will be free in the time of trouble and have no clogs to weigh them down. I saw that if any held on to their property and did not inquire of the Lord as to their duty, He would not make duty known, and they would be permitted to keep their property, and in the time of trouble it would come up before them like a mountain to crush them, and they would try to dispose of it, but would not be able (Early Writings, p. 56).

Again and again the Lord has instructed that our people are to take their families away from the cities, into the country, where they can raise their own provisions; for in the future the problem of buying and selling will be a very serious one (Country Living, pages 9-10).

But Why Must We Live In the Country?

We have not met with much resistance when delivering our country living message (in well over one hundred Seventh-day Adventist churches in diverse places), though we do hear some mild protests at times.

"Why do you think we should move out to the country? Our home was just remodeled. It's just the way we like it, now! It's finally comfortable."

"Living in the country is not very convenient; I know because I grew up that way—living from the garden, drawing water, chopping wood. I graduated and left that behind."

"Living in the country would put us way out of our comfort zone. We can easily keep up with our chore assignments here in the city. There wouldn't be much spare time in the country, would there?"

"My children need to go to school, and my husband's job is downtown."

Actually, if you are looking for an excuse to live in the city, it's not difficult to find one. It might even seem right. The problem is that while *we* might be able to give you some reasons, from our perspective, that *we* think you should move out of the city, God's requests and commands far outweigh our opinions. He tells us, more than once, that we *must* move out or possibly lose salvation!

In harmony with the light given me, I am urging people to come out from the great centers of population. Our cities are increasing in wickedness, and it is becoming more and more evident that those who remain in them unnecessarily do so at the peril of their soul's salvation (Country Living, *page 9*).

Although we may never know, in this life, all of God's reasons for asking of us that which we would not choose to do (or go, or be, or wear, or surrender), He *has* shared several practical reasons for moving out.

*Those who will take their families into the country, place them where they have fewer temptations. The children who are with parents that love and fear God, are in every way much better situated to learn of the Great Teacher, who is the source and fountain of wisdom. They have a much more favorable opportunity to gain a fitness for the kingdom of heaven. Send the children to schools located in the city, where every phase of temptation is waiting to attract and demoralize them, and the work of character building is **tenfold harder for both parents and children*** (Fundamentals of Christian Education, *p. 326: emphasis supplied*).

Can you think of a really good reason to postpone experiencing that tenfold advantage that we are promised will better prepare us for eternal life in a country setting?

Curtain Drawn Aside

Revelation 13:17 delineates a time in the near future when those who take a stand against the church/state power (the beast) that will rule the world, will not be able to buy anything, including food.

And that no man might buy or sell save he that had the mark, or the name of the beast, or the number of his name.

Accepting or rejecting the mark of the beast is an eternal decision. This decision will be strongly influenced by where we choose to live before this political power is established.

The Lord has shown me clearly that the image of the beast will be formed before probation closes; for it is to be the great test for the people of God, by which their eternal destiny will be decided (*Selected Messages*, book 2, p. 80).

Probationary time is preparation time. It is necessary to prepare safe places for our families outside the cities. Yet, according to 2 Chronicles 7:14, if the heart is not ready, even the work of our hands will not insure survival! What should we do? Where should we go? God has answers.

What Is "Country"?

"Where is *country*?" My husband, Jere, asks his audience at a typical *You Can Survive!* seminar. With the tone of an auctioneer, he then begins to ask for offers, "Who will give me five miles outside the city? Nobody? Ten miles? Who'll give me ten…?" Members of the audience look at each other with upraised eyebrows. A few hands are tentatively raised.

"Twenty miles…who'll give me twenty?" A few more hands are raised.

By the time Jere reaches thirty miles, most of the attendees allow that particular distance as a safe position to take.

"Sorry," Jere smiles, "That was a trick question, folks. Country is not a *place*, it's a *function*. If you can have your own well, raise a garden, have plenty elbow room, use an outhouse, burn wood, etc.—then you are *in the country*".

ABCs of Country Living—Seeking God's Character

After a few days at Sanctuary Ranch Family Camp guests will sometimes ask, "Are you going to teach a class in common sense? If you have one, I will come. I would feel better about moving out if I had been raised in the country, where we can better hear His voice of instruction."

Common sense is a way of looking at life. It is the essence of simplicity; the talent of being able to break a big problem into bite-sized pieces. *Simple* does not necessarily equate with *easy*. Common sense is the skill that enables us to do for ourselves what we would otherwise pay someone to do for us.

After finishing college, Jere experienced an all-consuming desire to learn the skills he did not obtain on the ball field, in college, or from his father. The more he read the Spirit of Prophecy, the more he realized he needed training in practical skills and in medical missionary work.

God wants the ministers and the church members to take a decided, active interest in the medical missionary work (Testimonies for the Church, vol. 6, p. 300).

Jere decided to go to Wildwood, a self-supporting, medical missionary training school. While there, Jere was assigned to live in Fred and Bessie Callahan's home. Fred was practical: he could lay tile, brick and block, was a good mechanic, grew the best watermelons, knew hydrotherapy, and had memorized an unlimited number of spiritual quotations appropriate to every occasion. Besides all this, Fred really loved his students and when he sensed Jere's interest in learning practical skills, he took a special interest in him.

One hot day, Jere was with Fred when his car got a flat tire. Fred showed Jere how to change it—himself. Jere wrestled with the tire for some time under the hot Georgia sun while Brother Callahan patiently watched his progress. Finally, Jere couldn't resist stating the obvious.

"Brother Callahan," Jere moped, "Can't we just take this flat tire down to the gas station?"

"We could, son," drawled the elderly gentleman, "But it's more important to get the man done than to get this job done."

The lesson stuck. When Jere had a son, he passed that concept on to Jed. I probably shouldn't brag, but, after witnessing so many mechanical miracles at Jed's hand, I tell anyone who will listen, "My son can fix anything, even without parts or tools!" Jed, now a certified organic grain grower, tells his Dad, "At least half of farming is knowing how to keep the equipment running!" I am so thankful that Jere chose a country setting in which to raise our son, and made sure he had tools, time, and a place to learn the practical skills necessary for his work. Whenever Jed's experiments didn't work, Jere just labelled it tuition. This attitude among parents encourages the development of common sense in their children.

What better investment can we make in our children's welfare than to teach them how to reason from cause to effect and to enjoy learning those practical skills that will stand them in good stead wherever they choose to go? A child who is familiar with the ABCs of true education, applying practical skills and solving problems through prayer is a survivor in the making.

The call to country living is a spiritual decision that affects every aspect of life. Involve your children from the beginning: the verification of need, prayer requests, the search for property, the move (he can donate toys to cut down clutter), and seeking the quiet life.

Parents can secure small homes in the country, with land for cultivation, where they can have orchards and where they can raise vegetables and small fruits to take the place of flesh meat, which is so corrupting to the life blood coursing through the veins. On such places the children will not be surrounded with the corrupting influences of city life. God will help His people to find such homes outside the cities (Medical Ministry, p. 310).

The Perfect Property

Although heaven is our real home, God is willing and able to find homes for the people who inquire—just ask the folks who sent us the stories in the book that you are reading! Until we find heaven, there are certain qualities that your property must possess, or it is not the answer to your prayer.

Agricultural Land: Even if you do not plan to have a market garden for income, you must have good soil in which you can grow a garden for home use. It is best to test your soil, or at least ask neighbors what kind of produce you can expect to grow.

Water: Rivers, lakes and creeks are nice, but a well with a hand pump is invaluable. A spring on a side hill above the house is ideal for gravity flow water to the house. Deep wells will work while electricity is available, but not when the solar grid stops functioning, or the electric bill cannot be paid. There are (non-electric) hand pumps available that will raise water down to a depth of 250 feet (Lehmans.com).

Wood: Even if you do not plan to cut lumber or build a log cabin for guests, you need fuel for heating and cooking. A good country property will have plenty of trees (that belong to you).

Air: Without good air quality, no matter what other good qualities our land may possess, it is not a safe environment. This usually means locating a piece of land far removed from an industrial center.

Note regarding property search and finances: Property which is not serviced by electricity, or has a difficult access, is usually much more affordable. Several families that we know lived in a camp trailer or fifth-wheel while their home was being built.

Learning Together

Some adults who have never had the chance to learn simple living, often enjoy acquiring a workable knowledge of building a cabin, cooking with wood, and taking a bath with water they have pumped from our well and heated over the fire at our family camp. But children seem to fall more naturally into simple survival habits. How fortunate is the child who is daily exposed to the joys of nature rather than the artificialities and unholy customs of the city. How much more wholesome to grow up learning to appreciate the power and goodness of nature's God. Children adapt. Sometimes parents resist change because it places more responsibility upon them for the education of their children.

"I have to live where my children can attend school," they might protest. Parents should consider the vicious customs and vices that pervade today's schools, and ask themselves, "Is it *safe* to send my child to school?" Remember that *tenfold* country advantage: *Send the children to schools located in the city, where every phase of temptation is waiting to attract and demoralize them, and the work of character building is **tenfold harder for both parents and children*** (*Fundamentals of Christian Education*, p. 326: emphasis supplied).

One of the greatest of the "tenfold advantages" a child will learn in the country school is how parents can help him focus beyond a "business as usual" approach to life. William Carey (self-supporting missionary to China) had a standard answer to inquiries about what he did for a living; "My business is serving the Lord; I cobble shoes to pay expenses." It is an important concept for a young child of God to learn that he is being groomed for eternity, not for time. By keeping in close touch with a child's schooling day by day, a parent can, with each lesson, lift the child's vision just a little higher.

Part of your research in planning a country move should be to learn which areas are home-school-friendly. It is safe to follow God's counsel. Parents can learn right along with their children about how to accomplish all things through the power of prayer. Lessons come harder with age, but none should ever feel they are beyond learning something new. Country living, like becoming a Christian, is a school from which one never graduates. Growing a garden in these last days will require the blessing of God.

If the land is cultivated, it will, with the blessing of God, supply our necessities (Country Living, p. 17).

How, exactly, do we get *the blessing of God* on our land? Growing a garden in the end times requires a specific type of preparation, more than just soil preparation.

If my people, which are called by my name, shall humble themselves, and pray, and seek my face, and turn from their wicked ways; then will I hear from heaven, and will forgive their sin, and will heal their land (2 Chronicles 7:14).

And I will rebuke the devourer for your sakes, and he shall not destroy the fruits of your ground; neither shall your vine cast her fruit before the time in the field, saith the LORD of hosts (Malachi 3:11).

Trimming Down

What is true in editing is true in moving; "less is more." It may well be that survival in end times will be more dependent on our ability to "get by" *without* than in being able to use what we have stored. Assess your real needs.

It is now that our brethren should be cutting down their possessions instead of increasing them. We are about to move to a better country, even a heavenly. Then let us not be dwellers upon the earth, but be getting things into as compact a compass as possible (Christian Service, p. 59: emphasis supplied).

Jere claims that stuff is "The Eighth Plague" and that it has already fallen. If you are willing, He will gently nudge you out of your attachments. Gone is any need of sentimental mementos. With the help of

Craig's List, Kijiji, thrift stores, consignment shops, and other great serv-ices, you may even receive payment for your unwanted "treasures" (see chapter 3, "Get Ready, Get Ready, Get Ready!")

Remind yourself, with each choice, that this world is not your home, you are moving away from your earthly home toward your heavenly home.

Simple Pleasures

Relocating is a great time to establish new traditions and increase en-thusiasm.

1) Make joyful occasions of meals, worships, and bedtime; main-tain a regular schedule.

2) Home business: know a skill whereby you can set your own hours, be your own boss, and make a viable living, maintain the discipline necessary to its success.

3) At every opportunity, use simple home remedies.

4) Outreach to neighbors and church friends, church evangelism; your country home is an outpost for city evangelism; *Said the mes-senger of God, "Shall not the cities be warned? Yes, not by God's people living in them, but by their visiting them, to warn them of what is com-ing upon the earth"* (*Evangelism*, p. 77).

5) Never stop growing: food, thankfulness, and character.

6) Simplify; electric appliances are good while we can "pay for the

plug", but begin to train your children to get by without electricity by having "back up systems" in place. Practice together, once a month, an electric-free-day, where the whole family does without electricity as much as possible: write letters, wash clothes on a scrub board, cut wood with your crosscut or bow saw, bake a batch of bread in the wood cook stove, do crafts (knitting, crocheting, art work, use hand tools to do repairs), play music (non-electric instruments), exercise, and use candles (safely). Parents, make these activities an opportunity for togetherness; God enjoys unity. Most children enjoy nothing more than interacting with their parents in a stress-free environment.

Pressing Together

One very cold December night we were awakened to the wind howling through the trees. Before breakfast time, we were without electricity. We were really in the dark, since the sun does not come up until close to 11 AM during Canada's North Country winters. We lit some candles and the wood cook stove, and stoked the heater. We had morning worship by candlelight and were soon enjoying our usual Sunday morning feast of pancakes and fruit. Throughout the day, we used the outhouse instead of the indoor toilet, melted snow for our water, and rescheduled our day. Inspection of our grounds revealed that the porch swing had landed in the back yard among other pieces of porch furniture. The dogs were excited to be with us as we patrolled the rest of our acreage.

On the way home, we stopped at the root cellar to get some potatoes. In pulling the door shut, Jere injured his hand. Rather than go to the hospital, we washed his skinned hand with soap, poured peroxide on it, and then placed a large bandage over it. After a simple lunch of Borscht (canned the previous year) and crackers, we used the remainder of the day for editing (this very book!). Our gift-daughter, Kenya, actually finished her Medical Missionary Home Study Course from MEET Ministries on that very day, though she had to wait for electricity to send in her tests via e-mail. For evening worship we played music (piano and guitar) and sang, then read our spiritual reading by candlelight. Although we were not able to finish the list we had planned for the day, we were able to accomplish, without fear, what we needed to do.

Preparation removes fear. Be ready. The essence of country living is learning to cope with emergencies without fear. "Use it up, wear it out, make it do, or do without!" Practice "getting by." Self-denial is a strong building block for a godly character. Simple living requires a pressing together of the family unit, not by force but with goal-oriented unity.

Plan Ahead

If you are a parent, plan some quality time with your children *without electricity* each day; story time, a walk, gardening (with object lessons), a learning game, etc. Today there is the temptation to let "toys" replace parental time. Enjoy your children; they are the Lord's blessing, not an interruption. Reinforce their positive character traits. Exchange condemnation for hands-on affection whenever possible. Avoid the pitfalls of indulgence and sentimentality, but never lose an opportunity to demonstrate love. If your children know they are appreciated, they will become joyful little workers and want to be with you. Is there any higher calling than raising a child?

There is a God above, and the light and glory from His throne rests upon the faithful mother as she tries to educate her children to resist the influence of evil. No other work can equal hers in importance. She has not, like the artist, to paint a form of beauty upon canvas; nor, like the sculptor, to chisel it from marble. She has not, like the author, to embody a noble thought in words of power; nor, like the musician, to express a beautiful sentiment in melody. It is hers, with the help of God, to develop in a human soul the likeness of the divine. (*Adventist Home*, p. 237).

No One Left Behind

There is only one thing to fear for the future:

We have nothing to fear for the future, except as we shall forget the way the Lord has led us, and His teaching in our past history (*Selected Messages*, book 3, p. 162).

There are varied reasons that people fear a move to the country. Some become concerned about their inability to be productive: they have health problems, various restrictions, are on medications, or other, multi-faceted and "unsolvable" problems. Some are truly afraid of the dark, or wild animals. Considering a move to the country petrifies them! Don't fear to pray about the problem. God has solutions, and He specializes in the slightly impossible!

The Lord specializes in removing fear. One fear that surfaces most often is the knowledge of limitations. They are only one; they cannot do the move to the country alone. This fear helps drive us together, to depend on one another for survival. We suggest that single people, the aged, those with special challenges, become part of a group effort. As each person contributes what they can (financially, physically, spiritually) the group is strengthened.

"No one is left behind," Jere says. He points to an elderly widow in the front row at a large seminar in the eastern US and asks, "Tell me, ma'am, what can you do?"

"I can't do *anything*… well, I can make bread," she shrugs.

"You're on *my* team!" Jere says with a smile. "Brothers and Sisters, none of us can do everything that needs to be done, neither are many of us able to do what we used to do, but, with a willing heart we all have something worthwhile to contribute. The important thing is to do what God would have us to, by His might and in His Spirit. No one is left behind."

We have differing talents. Some folks have only a couple of skills they can pass along. Others seem to be able to do many things, but those who "make it through" will be found sharing what they have, helping each other overcome fear. In the strength of the Holy Spirit, we will overcome; not by strength, nor by skill, but by surrender.

What did God ask Moses when he sent him to guide His people away from Egypt? Did He ask Moses if he had a plan whereby he could organize those uncultured slaves into a smoothly operating group? No, He merely asked, "What is that in thine hand?" (Exodus 4:2) God used what he had, a simple shepherd's staff. And so it is today; God uses that which we dedicate to him. Each of us has something in our hand that can be a blessing if it is dedicated to God. Someone may have land. Someone else has tools. Another person knows gardening and cooking skills. Survival will require a concerted effort. There is not one person who has all the skills necessary to surviving the end times. We will survive…together. Survival is sharing.

By this shall all men know that ye are my disciples, if ye have love one to another (John 13:35).

Courage or Cowardice?

We sometimes hear this statement in our seminars, "It's a cowardly Christian who will leave the city when there are so many people who need our witness! Those who move to the country are running from duty!"

Consider the destruction of Jerusalem. Were there not people living there who needed salvation? Yes, but time ran out. God asked them to leave before judgments fell on that city. It was their only safety.

Christ gave His disciples a sign of the ruin to come on Jerusalem, and He told them how to escape: "When ye shall see Jerusalem compassed with armies, then know that the desolation thereof is nigh. Then let them which are in Judea flee to the mountains; and let them which are in the midst of it depart out; and let not them that are in the countries enter thereinto. For these be the days of vengeance, that all things which are written may be fulfilled." This warning was given to be heeded forty years after, at the destruction of Jerusalem. The Christians obeyed the warning, and **not a Christian perished** *in the fall of the city* (The Desire of Ages, p. 630).

Not one Christian perished in the destruction of Jerusalem! Why? Because they weren't there! They heeded Christ's warning. They left!

As God's commandment-keeping people we **must leave the cities**. *As did Enoch, we must work in the cities but not dwell in them. The cities are to be worked from outposts. Said the messenger of God, "Shall not the cities be warned? Yes, not by God's people living in them but by their visiting them, to warn them of what is coming upon the earth"* (Last Day Events, p. 96).

According to Scripture Lot made more than one mistake, but his greatest was in thinking to make an impression for good on his erring friends and neighbors by living among them. Enoch was instructed how to work the cities of his day. This wisdom also applies.

He [Enoch] did not locate in Sodom, thinking to save Sodom. He placed himself and his family where the atmosphere would be as pure as possible (*Seventh-day Adventist Bible Commentary*, E. G. White Comments, vol. 1, p. 1087).

God's invitation to country living is a summons to build a refuge. Country living is not meant to be an escape from duty. He asks us to be willing, as was Enoch, to raise our family outside the city, training our children God's way, that we may have the courage to demonstrate His love to a world in need. We are to establish safe places outside the cities where we can better prepare for eternal life away from worldly influences.

I-Pod for a Pea Pod?

After hearing the seminar we presented in Texas, 16-year-old Wes determined to spend a summer with us. His family could not help him with the cost of transportation. Wes had one prized possession—an I-pod, which he sold to his uncle for the price of a round-trip bus ticket. He was a full four days and nights on the bus from Dallas to Chetwynd. When our phone rang, I saw that it was from a local pay phone. A quiet voice said, "I'm here."

I asked his name, his current location, and assured him we would be right there to pick him up. Wes did not just find his way to our home, he stepped right into our hearts. He spent the summer helping bring in the hay, lifting heavy bales of dirt and big patio pots in the greenhouse, he weeded and picked raspberries, played the piano, drove the quad, walked our trails, swam in the river, and shelled an abundance of peas. Wes had a good appetite, but his greatest hunger was for country living and discovering God's will for his life.

Jere says of Wes and his exhausting bus ride to our home in northern British Columbia, "Wes traded his I-pod for a pea pod!"

Will it come down to that for all of us? Looking at the no buy-no sell situation, a scoop of peas will look mighty good when our electronics are all dead! Ask the Lord to help you find His way of escape to your promised home in the country! It will cost each of us something, but whatever the price of preparation, heaven will be cheap enough!

"What Shall I Do For Income?"

Not more surely is the place prepared for us in the heavenly mansions than is the special place designated on earth where we are to work for God (*Christ's Object Lessons*, p. 326).

There are few more important decisions we will make in life than our choice of occupation. "Who will I serve, and how?" Remember William Carey's comment on his work? "My business is serving the Lord, I cobble shoes to pay expenses." If you put God first, He will show you what to do to pay expenses.

We recommend that young people not marry until they know their work. How would a young man know which car to buy unless he knows where he will be driving? How will he know who should go with him until he knows where he is going? If he chooses to live in the country, he will need a practical wife who knows how to improvise. God has a work for each of us to do, enjoyable work that contributes significantly to the good of humanity.

Before our son, Jed, was married, he discussed his life work with us. "If someone discovers a work that they really enjoy, then they never have to work a day in their life! Maybe that's how God helps us find the work He wants us to do." Jed became an organic grain farmer and his dear wife, raised on a Montana farm, loves driving tractor!

Consider what you enjoy doing. If it can glorify God, then build a business around it. Some people use this to direct their move to an area where their services are in demand. Explore the market. Certain hobbies can become a working business (crafts, unfortunately, rarely pay for the time spent in making them).

There are unlimited advantages to working from home. Though it requires some self-discipline to maintain a schedule, working at home leaves opportunity for Dad to be home for lunch, and take a day off when the need arises. Whether you work at home or elsewhere, it is best to be self-employed; you can set your own hours, be able to spend more time in the garden during the growing season, and you never have to be entangled in a union.

The trades unions and confederacies of the world are a snare. Keep out of them, and away from them, brethren. Have nothing to do with them. Because of these unions and confederacies, it will soon be very difficult for our institutions to carry on their work in the cities. My warning is: Keep out of the cities. (Country Living, p. 10).

The wicked are being bound up in bundles, bound up in trusts, in unions, in confederacies. Let us have nothing to do with these organizations (*Last Day Events*, p. 116).

Some folks are better at marketing goods, others at creating them. Use your talents wisely; depend on someone else to do the marketing if you are weak, but work on improving weaknesses after someone helps you find buyers and set prices. Charge a reasonable fee; don't give away your goods and services, but be consistent with your pricing.

No business will work unless someone keeps the paperwork up-to-date. Be careful to pay your taxes; freedom, while it lasts, is worth supporting. Whatever business you decide to do, no job is actually finished until the paperwork is done. Have a simple bookkeeping system and keep your billings and receipts orderly. This is a great teaching tool for your children as they see you being careful to detail.

In the home the child is to be taught the importance of neatness, order, and thoroughness, and these lessons are to be repeated in the school (*Manuscript Releases,* vol. 10, p. 324).

Home-Based Industries

The possibilities for self-employment are limited only by imagination! Listed here are a few industries that might spark your interest if you are not yet self-employed. This is not meant to be a complete list; it is a springboard for research!

- ♦ Accountant
- ♦ Animals: farrier, grooming, walking, kennel
- ♦ Architecture
- ♦ Auto Body and/or Detailing
- ♦ Baking

- Bee-keeping
- Business Plan Service
- Call center representative
- Carpentry: cabinets, roofing, contracting
- Catering: food specialties
- Cleaning Service: house, window, carpet
- Computer: virtual tutor, virtual assistant, web developer, programmer
- Consulting and Placement Services
- Colporteur work
- Craft Business
- Detailing (cars and trucks)
- Electrical
- Engineering
- Farmer's Market
- Farming
- Financial Planner
- Furniture
- Greenhouse; bedding, baskets, containers
- Hair Care
- Heavy Equipment
- Herbal: salves, essential oil
- Interior Design
- Landscaping
- Lessons: specialty skills, music, art, etc.
- Laundry
- Market Gardening
- Masonry: brick, block, tile
- Massage Therapy
- Medical Missionary Work

- Medical and paramedical fields
- Mechanic
- Mushrooms
- Music Lessons
- Natural Cosmetics: soap, lotion, shampoo, laundry soap
- Nursing
- Organizer
- Painting: interior and exterior
- Personal Trainer
- Photography, videography
- Physical Therapy
- Plumbing
- Real Estate
- Reseller; second hand
- Sewing: mending (industrial coveralls, etc.), embroidering (specialized logos), knitting
- Snow Removal
- Tax Preparer
- Technical support specialist
- Tilling (customized gardens)
- Transcriber
- Translator
- Travel agent
- Tree Farm
- Trucking
- Upholstering
- Wallpaper hanging
- Welding
- Windows; replace, clean, seasonal painting
- Writer/Editor

Another Ark to Build

That ark cost Noah everything he had. All of his time and money was tied up in his assignment; preaching about the coming storm while he worked on God's escape plan for his family and anyone who wanted to be saved from destruction. Many there were as it began to rain, who wished they had answered Noah's invitation instead of laughing at what appeared, to their short-sighted vision, to be the senseless rants of a foolish old man.

*"By faith Noah, being warned of God of things not seen as yet, moved with fear, prepared an ark to the saving of his house; by the which he condemned the world, and became heir of the righteousness which is by faith." Hebrews 11:7. While Noah was giving his warning message to the world, his works testified of his sincerity. It was thus that his faith was perfected and made evident. He gave the world an example of believing just what God says. **All that he possessed, he invested in the ark**. As he began to construct that immense boat on dry ground, multitudes came from every direction to see the strange sight and to hear the earnest, fervent words of the singular preacher. **Every blow struck upon the ark was a witness to the people** (Patriarchs and Prophets, p. 95).*

It's a question worth asking ourselves each day, "What blow can I strike today in order witness to the people around me?" Country living is not a call to fun and games. It's a call to a structured, healthy, productive lifestyle. It is preparation for the relentless marathon against the storm that will soon sweep the earth. From the twenty-fifth floor downtown, God calls us to the country, then, eventually, to the wilderness, and finally to heaven. It is our call, each day, to take another step toward heaven and away from the things of earth.

God has always given men warning of coming judgments. Those who had faith in His message for their time, and who acted out their faith, in obedience to His commandments, escaped the judgments that fell upon the disobedient and unbelieving. The word came to Noah, "Come thou and all thy house into the ark; for thee have I seen righteous before me." Noah obeyed and was saved. The message came to Lot, "Up, get you out of this place; for the Lord will destroy this city." Gen. 7:1; 19:14. Lot placed himself under the guardianship of the heavenly messengers, and was saved. So Christ's disciples were given warning of the destruction of Jerusalem. Those who watched for the sign of the coming ruin, and fled from the city, escaped the destruction. So now we are given warning of Christ's second coming and of the destruction to fall upon the world. Those who heed the warning will be saved (Maranatha, p. 36).

We see people taking the invitation to country living seriously. It is God's ark for the future. The following stories are modern day miracles of how God provided country homes for those who took Him at His word.

God will help His people to find such homes outside of the cities (Medical Ministry, p. 310).

TWO

Gift of Jehovah

PIPER IVINS

Speak unto the children of Israel, that they go forward.
Exodus 14:15

We first met Stan and Piper at a seminar we were presenting in New Jersey several years ago. When we heard them singing together, with Piper playing her guitar and Stanley accompanying on his harmonica, we asked if they could sing special music for the weekend series. From the very beginning, there was the sense that our friendship had been waiting to happen. As their story unfolds, you will understand that God intervened in their "escape to the country." There is no denying their direct answers to prayer. There were numerous problems to keep them from being able to relocate, such as debts and lack of employment. But they believed that it was time for them to be in the country and that there was a plan for them to find their home. That is the attitude in which they went in search of a country home. Here, Piper tells their amazing story—the incident that she and Stan refer to as their "Red Sea experience."

Once again we found ourselves camping in our van in the mountains of West Virginia. Stanley, my husband, still lost in thought, stared into the crackling fire, wondering, daring to hope, if tomorrow would bring us closer to our dream of moving to the country to raise our children away from worldly enticements.

"Piper, maybe I'm feeling like Abraham felt," Stanley puzzled aloud. "God has called me out, but where?"

There could be no doubt that the hand of providence had guided Stanley and me, and we couldn't help sensing that God was orchestrating "something big" once more. Never, not in our wildest dreams, could we have imagined just how big and how soon He would work!

Dreaming of Escape

For several years we attended family camp meetings, read *Country Living* and other Spirit of Prophecy books, dreaming of the day we would "escape." It seemed every book we read and every sermon we heard pointed us to the soon coming of Jesus. We wanted to be prepared to meet Him. We did what we could, clinging fast to our dream of the day we could "escape" and begin to prepare our country outpost. After we attended a workshop by Jere Franklin, we felt an even stronger sense of urgency and prayed daily that God would lead us to that special place He had set aside for us.

We contemplated southern Pennsylvania, Virginia, West Virginia, and western Maryland. West Virginia became the most logical choice for several reasons, but particularly because land prices were more reasonable. Stanley had experience in the construction trade, so we decided to look for something on which we could afford a small down payment, and be able to remodel it over time. I especially leaned toward old farmhouses because they possess so much character. We combed the easterly counties of West Virginia, searching for "the place." Would we know it when we saw it?

Stanley would jest as we traveled, "Darlin', one of these days we are going to drive down some dead end road and there it will be! The place God has saved for us with a big halo over the house! I don't know how we'll know, but I believe that when we see it God will reveal it in His own way!" Eight months later, still no halos. And here we were, camping in the van, again.

The next day found Stanley, on the job, discussing our fruitless property search with his Best Friend. In his construction business, he frequently works alone and often holds audible conversations with his Maker.

"We're spending a lot of time and money driving around getting nowhere, Lord." He sighed as he laid down his hammer. "We really need some direction here."

The previous weekend we had traveled, unintentionally, through a quaint little town by the name of Mathias. It was too far south. Or was it? After he prayed for guidance, Stanley was immediately impressed with the thought, "Mathias is the place to look!" He burst through the door that evening with a new plan.

"Piper, the Lord gave me direction! On my way home I bought a West Virginia Gazetteer!" We spread out the map on the dining room table and drew a ten mile radius around the little town of Mathias.

That next weekend, following our new plan, we returned to the beautiful state park we had visited just five days earlier, whose atmosphere soothed my soul. The park lies in a hollow with tall pines and a creek running beside the road. We felt as if we were driving through a picture postcard. We ascended a winding, mountain road, past some comfortable-looking country homes and arrived on the upper ridge. Realizing the lateness of the hour, we decided to go just far enough down this road so that we could safely turn around. Suddenly, through a large break in the trees, there appeared a breathtaking view of a beautiful, fertile valley. Stanley stopped the car and leaned on the steering wheel. We absorbed the beauty in a reverent silence.

"What a beautiful place to build a house," I thought to myself.

Stanley shook his head and commented facetiously, "Wouldn't it be just miserable to have to live here?"

Checking the time he said, "It's almost four o'clock! Let's just go a little further down this road and if we don't see anything we'll head for home." We had no choice but to continue as there was nowhere to easily turn around on the narrow road. Shortly thereafter, we came to a beautifully constructed four-board fence such as one would see on a farm in a calendar picture. The enclosed hill sloped down to a weathered, old farm house.

Dream House

"Look honey," I said pointing down the hill. "There's an old farmhouse down there! It looks abandoned!"

"Take a look at the fence! We couldn't even afford to buy that!"

I couldn't take my eyes off of the house. It felt like the Lord was impressing me to pursue the matter. Following the fence line past the driveway, we saw two stone piers and an iron gate with a padlock. Stanley noticed that on one pillar a stone mason had worked an "S". The other post held the letter "P".

"Look, Piper!" Stanley grinned playfully, "This must be the place the Lord has for us. Our initials are already in stone!"

I hadn't even noticed the initials. My heart was intent on inquiring of the Lord, "Could this be *the place*?" We went farther up the road, turned around, and headed for home. We approached the farm again.

"Stanley," I urged, placing my hand on his arm, "I'd like to go down and look at the house." There were no signs that said NO TRESPASSING, and I just had to take a peek. "You don't have to come. You can stay and read your book if you want."

Though there wasn't a cow in sight, Stanley capitalized on the evidence at hand in an attempt to prevent further exploration. He shook his head seriously, but I saw the twinkle in his eye.

"There's probably a bull hiding in that ancient barn over there! He might chase you!" That thought deterred me for all of two seconds, then I proceeded to exit the vehicle. The children tumbled out as well, thankful to stretch their legs. So, here we all are, walking down this long sloping hill to an old abandoned farm house, set in a "holler" (as West Virginians call the valley floor), walking over dried cow pies, and a multitude of large stones. I can't hide my excitement. Here is a beautiful, quiet setting: the house, the two old run-down barns one of which has the "Detroit lean," a shed that appears to have a root cellar built beneath it, a number of fruit trees on the hillside, and two large, spring-fed concrete water cisterns.

Stanley kept looking back over his shoulder, expressing concern that

someone might see us and send a truckload of "hillbillies" with guns to run us off the place. We took notice of the roof line, walls, windows, and the mortar and stone foundation. The exterior siding was weather-beaten white and some of the boards were bowed with nails extruding from them. Much of the wood was rotted away along the fascia, rake board, and soffit. Yes, it appeared sound, but it needed a hefty amount of cosmetic renovation, and a lot of TLC. By then we had reached the dilapidated porch. One of the pillars had pulled away from its base and was dangling, and several floor boards were missing.

The screen door was locked, but the interior door was ajar. We sent our youngest son through a window (missing its pane of glass), and he simply let us in through the front door. I have seen some pretty big messes in my lifetime, but nothing to equal what had been left in that old house! Old furniture was strewn across outdated, orange shag carpet and well-used linoleum in the living and dining rooms, but the exposed joists in the ceiling of these two rooms were an attribute I particularly liked. They had been painted turquoise, but I knew that I could restore them to their original beauty. The doors were painted dark brown. What color combinations! In the bathroom, soiled insulation dangled through a large hole in the ceiling. Muddy paw prints making pathways through numerous holes in the walls and ceiling indicated a leaky roof. The icing on the bacterial cake was discovered in the mud/laundry room where we teetered across the rotted floor, ducked under collapsed drywall and filthy insulation, to where it joined with what was left of the aforementioned bathroom wall and floor. Old metal cabinets in the kitchen were streaked with animal waste, but the size of the room was easily large enough for our family of five. The large pantry, a separate room off of the kitchen, was ideal. Yes, it was filthy, but what potential!

Upstairs, by way of a "servant's stairway," construction typical of that era, we discovered four bedrooms with a large open hallway where we could take a larger stairway back down to the living room. The rooms were a comfortable size, but had no closets. This lack appeared to have been remedied in a unique manner with a large community closet in the hallway. Our three children were very excited at the aspect of having their own rooms. We had not known, until that day, that this would be an answer to their prayer! The ceiling, floor and walls were all tongue and groove boards. Some rooms had a heavy canvas wall covering and exterior walls that were not insulated. I loved the fact that everything was made of wood with no plaster or other material on the walls of the original house. The light switches were an old push-button kind that I had never seen before. I loved them, but suspected that they would have to be replaced.

I stood in the living room looking out on the green meadows. Was this what the Lord had in store for us? A great love and respect for the old homestead welled up in my heart. Promises flooded my mind: God owns the cattle on a thousand hills. All things are possible with Him. Then and there, I determined to discover the owner.

"Stanley, can we handle a project this big?" I asked my husband who was still intent on watching the driveway for sharpshooters. I interpreted semi-optimism in the shrug of his shoulders. When I told him I was ready to go, he was visibly relieved and hastily funneled us through the front door and up the hill to the car.

"I'd like to find out more about this house, Honey" I insisted.

"If you want to waste your time chasing this jackrabbit, you go right ahead," Stanley said.

Good Dreams Need a Foundation

The chase was on. I was like a racehorse flying out of the starting gate. I couldn't wait to find some answers. On our way through Mathias we stopped in at a store and inquired about this property. We received a little historical information, but no answer as to ownership.

Arriving home, I called a realtor and explained our discovery. She was intrigued. Two days later, she gave me phone numbers for the owner and for the property manager. I quickly dialed the owner's number and left a message. When I reached the manager, he listened patiently as I explained our discovery. Then I inquired if he might know whether the owner would be interested in someone living on his property while fixing up the house. He said that the owner was away, but that he would check with him and get back to me.

I waited patiently (somewhat), but when the weekend arrived and I still hadn't heard from him, I called back.

"Sorry," He apologized. "I've been a little busy. Yes, the owner is interested." He then suggested we go back out to the house and take a close look at the work that needed to be done and make sure we'd want to tackle such a large project because the house had been vacant for many years. He went on to explain that a few years earlier, someone had tried and had become overwhelmed in only two weeks.

The next weekend we headed back to the "holler" to document, video-tape, investigate, and list the jobs to be done as we envisioned the project. After considering the many repairs needed, Stanley and I decided that, with the Lord's help, we could accomplish the task of transforming the house into a livable dwelling. While in Mathias, we phoned the property manager to arrange a meeting with him that day. He declined saying that he didn't want to proceed any further without the owner's approval. He suggested that we mail him a couple letters of reference. That was not what I wanted to hear! I wilted like a deflated balloon, but I tried not to let my feelings ruin the day. I was just so anxious to get started!

"Sweetheart," Stanley enfolded me in a gentle, loving embrace when he noticed the tears in my eyes that afternoon, "If it's the Lord's will for us to be there, it'll all work out." Those were the words that encouraged me to trust God's leading.

I was again encouraged as I considered the sequence of events—discovering the ideal country location, our family all in unity on accomplishing the project, the possibility of the owner being interested in our proposal. It seemed too wonderful a dream to be laid aside. Besides, I am not one to be diverted easily, and my faith was growing daily since our discovery. If ever I'd had "evidence of things not seen" (but dreamed of), it was this farm! But it needed some major attention to become our "substance of things hoped for" before winter.

This had all transpired over Memorial Day weekend 2005. Early the next day, at the close of my Tuesday morning devotional time, I sought affirmation from the Lord.

"Lord, if it's your will for us to be in that house, please let me know sometime this week. There's so much preparation to be made before winter."

The Miracle

It was a normal day with Stanley being off to work by 7 AM, and the rest of us preparing to start home school for the day. As I was helping one of our daughters with her workbook, the phone rang. It was the owner of the property!

"I understand you've been out to see my place."

"Oh yes!" I answered. "We have been driving all around this area of West Virginia looking for a place in the country. We want to simplify our lifestyle and we really like the beautiful location of your farm."

He began interviewing me on the phone asking many questions about my personal background, my husband's background, both of our parents, what we did for a living.

"And where do you intend to send your children to school?" When I explained that we home-schooled our children, he seemed pleased.

"Good! I wouldn't recommend you put your children in public school there. By the way, are you Christians?"

"Yes."

"What denomination?" I hesitated, wondering if his religious experience had been positive or negative. I swallowed hard, breathed a fervent prayer, and answered as calmly as I could, "Seventh-day Adventist."

His voice brightened. "Oh! I know several Adventists. I have the fondest memories of a lady who was a very dear friend of my mother. She was a Seventh-day Adventist. My grandmother was in an Adventist hospital and they took such good care of her. I've known quite a few Adventists, myself. You all appear to be hardworking, honest people."

I breathed a sigh of relief, but the best was yet to come.

"Hey, aren't you folks the ones who put out those Bible Story Books that you see in the doctors' offices?"

"Yes we are."

"I used to have a set of those books, but I gave them away. I've regretted it ever since! I've been trying to find a set for the last ten years, but with no success."

"Well, they still print them."

"Yeah, but I don't like the new ones." I could hear his frown. "I like the ones based on the King James Version of the Bible. The new ones don't have the poetry of the older ones."

"I believe I have a set of the old ones."

"Really?"

"Yes, they were given to our children by my father," I said. "Let me go get one." So I ran to get a book and sure enough, the publishing date was 1953 and it was the King James Version. I read him a line from the book along with the publishing date. His voice became reverent.

"You know, Piper, everything I know about the Bible I learned from those books. I can still see the pictures in my mind." After a pause he continued, "Well, I'll tell you what; if you could find it in your heart to let me have those books, I'll let you have my house."

I covered my mouth as it dropped open in astonishment. My morning prayer washed over me like sunshine, "Lord, if it's your will for us to be in that house, please let me know sometime this week…." Tears welled up in my eyes. I had trouble controlling my voice as I shared my morning prayer with this kind stranger.

"Oh, so you're the one who 'summoned' me today?" he chuckled.

I asked him some questions about the house and why it hadn't been occupied. He told me that he had bought it at an estate auction when the owner died. He had grown up in this area of West Virginia and didn't want to lose these country properties to developers, so when they come up for sale, he buys them to keep them preserved. This one happened to have a house, which meant nothing to him other than it could serve as a storage building, but that if it would suffice for us to make a home in it that we could go right ahead and do with it whatever we wanted; to fix it up however it pleased us.

"You can live there rent-free. Just take care of it as if it were your own. If you take care of my things, I'll take care of you."

I couldn't thank him enough for the offer and I knew at that point, God was in this and I had no fear of moving forward. This meant giving our notice to our landlord, have a yard sale and start packing. We went from not knowing where we were going to actually moving in two weeks time. Talk about a swift move! When God begins to answer a prayer, we need to fasten our seat belts!

As we were packing and having our yard sale that first weekend, the owner called and asked us if we had a place to stay while we worked on the house, because he had another farmhouse about four miles down the road that we would be welcome to stay in if we so desired. I was floored again! Not only did he offer us one house, now he was offering two! I felt doubly affirmed by God. We had already made arrangements with my dad to borrow his camping trailer to set in the yard while we were preparing this house, so I declined his offer, telling him how very much I appreciated his thoughtfulness. I then proceeded to bound out the door to share with Stanley that phone conversation. He assured me that it would have been too much work to maintain both homes while fixing the one.

Or Was It a Miracle?

We had set a date of June tenth to meet with the owner and his property manager to get acquainted and go over the details of where we wanted to start renovating the house. We had to complete the transaction, so, with our precious cargo, The Bible Story Books, tucked protectively into our load, we left for wild, wonderful, West Virginia. We arrived at "our" gate and waited… and waited… and waited. As time passed, doubts tried to take root in Stanley's mind.

What if this whole thing falls through? You have quit your job. You gave the landlord notice. You could be unemployed and homeless!

Then, replaying the events of the past few days, he dismissed the thoughts as those of the enemy trying to plant seeds of doubt. He knew full well the Lord was in this. Just as Stanley sent Satan packing, an old truck pulled in behind us.

At last, the property manager arrived and told us that the owner of the property was stuck in traffic outside of DC and would be here as soon as possible. He was instructed to take us over to the second house to see if we changed our minds about staying there, while fixing this one. As we toured, he explained that this house hadn't been occupied for twenty years or so. It is a historic home where the Tusing sisters used to live, which happened to be the property manager's great aunts. They were Mennonite women who lived like the pioneers in a modern world. They had no electricity, no running water, and they cooked on a wood cook stove. They had a milk cow, laying hens, grew their own veggies and had fruit trees. They also made their own clothes and were famous in this area for their weaving skills of fabrics and rugs. (We later obtained an interesting documentary of their story by the Smithsonian Institute.)

We returned to the house in which we were interested, and waited for the owner. When he emerged from his vehicle, I was surprised to see a middle-aged man who looked so very down-to-earth in his corduroy pants, button-down oxford shirt and a baseball cap on his graying head. I guess I was expecting someone in a business suit. What a pleasure it was to meet him! I felt like running up to him and giving him a big hug to thank him, but somehow that didn't seem quite appropriate. I felt as if we had discovered a long-lost uncle. With such overwhelming gratitude, it was hard to keep from displaying my emotions as we completed our introductions!

Together we walked around the house and then through it, discussing our vision with the owner. At the close of the tour the owner looked at us and smiled.

"This is your house. Fix it up as nice as you want it."

Kind Gestures

Immediately I envisioned the house, in God's time, restored to its original beauty. I also pictured my loving Father desiring to restore His image in me.

"The first thing I'd like to do is rewire the house," Stanley was saying. "The wiring is ancient. If we are getting into the walls to do that, it would make sense to insulate the walls and replace the windows at the same time."

"Well, Stanley," the owner explained, "This is like a dance; we're learning to dance together. You try not to step on my toes and I'll not step on yours. I do everything in cash. I do not deal in credit, so if the money's not there, then it has to wait until there is some. You came at me out of the blue and to be quite honest with you there is no money in this year's budget for you."

Even though we had no guarantee of insulation, or electricity, we were at least in agreement that we would just have to do the best we could with what we had. At first we were disappointed, but the Lord had proved that He would not abandon us, over and over again. We knew that He would get us through the cold winter months.

"Come on outside," said the owner as he opened the door for us. "There are cows on the property from May through November, so we need to fence the yard. How large a yard do you need? How large should we make the yard?" We mapped out an area we thought would be sufficient, but he enlarged our play space when we mentioned how much we like to play outside with our children. He instructed the property manager to start construction on the fence by Monday (this was Friday).

"Do you like to garden?"

"Yes!" We all responded enthusiastically. "It's one of the main reasons we want to be in the country!"

He showed us the garden spot and told the property manager to have it plowed up for us by the time we moved into the house. In addition, he explained that there were many fruit trees on the hillside to enjoy: apple, peach, cherry, and pear. There was also an old apple orchard just beyond the house.

"They are all yours!" He motioned with a generous sweep of his arms. "Just don't let them go to waste."

If he had rolled out a red carpet I couldn't have felt more welcomed! To myself, I said over and over, "Lord, what have we done to receive all this kindness?"

We left that day knowing that we had a mountain of work to do, but we were in good spirits. God had made it plain that this was the place he had reserved for us. I had to trust that He would work out the technicalities—in His time.

When I checked with the electric company about hooking up service to the house, I was informed that an inspection would be required first. The next week I met the electrical inspector to see about getting service. He told me that the wiring in the house was not just old, it was antiquated. He didn't want to pass it, but said he would if we made rewiring the house top priority, because it really was not safe. When I gave the owner the electrical report he surprised me.

"I will be in town again on the weekend of July 4th," he responded. "Have your list of materials and their cost ready for me then."

I spent the remainder of that day in a series of praises to God for moving upon the owner's heart to allow us to start to insulate and rewire the house before January! We had stepped out in faith, and the Lord had provided! Just as Moses had led the children of Israel through the Red Sea by his great faith in God, we were feeling that this was our Red Sea experience. It was a massive demonstration to us, His children, that He would protect, lead, and provide for our needs. We felt all of these things from our Heavenly Father in a very real and personal way. July 1st was our official moving day. We had much to do, but nothing seemed insurmountable, now.

On one occasion, when I moved a load of our belongings out to our "new" home in the country, the owner was there waiting for us. While I descended the long driveway, I noticed that he was doing something around the smaller barn. I pulled into the driveway as he smiled and opened the gate.

"Welcome home!" He said, "I just wanted to be here to welcome you to your new home. I hope you don't mind that I used your string-trimmer, but I thought I'd make myself useful until you arrived, by cleaning up some of this tall grass around the barn."

"We don't mind at all!" I assured him. "We certainly appreciate your efforts! Sorry we weren't here sooner!"

"No problem! I also brought something for your garden. Do you like tomatoes?" He asked as he turned and walked over to the trunk of his vehicle and pulled out a beautiful, healthy-looking tomato plant.

"What a kind gesture!" I thought as I received the plant and thanked him for everything he had done for us, including the "dance" we were learning.

Engraved In Stone

The Lord works in various ways to convey His love to us. Sometimes he uses people to speak to us for Him. I felt like Jesus, himself, was welcoming us to the place he had intended for us all along. This house had been vacant for fifteen years. We are only the third family to inhabit this beautiful 240 acre farm, since the house had been built back in the early 1900's. The stone piers at the top of our driveway were built with the "P" and the "S" on them before Stanley and I even knew each other. I can't help but think that the Lord may have smiled to Himself as the stone mason laid our initials in the gate posts. "Won't Stanley and Piper be surprised to see their initials on this place that I've reserved for them?"

Upon inquiry of the letters on the stone piers, the owner explained that they were the initials of his twin daughters.

"You might think that that's what those initials stand for," Stanley winked, "But I know what they really mean!"

"I think you might be right!" The owner smiled and chuckled softly.

God was planning our future long before we felt our need; even before Stanley and I had met! How awesome He is! He has fulfilled His promises to us. The Holy Spirit prepared us to receive the gift He had planned. We have immensely enjoyed the beauty, wildlife, and serenity of our new home. It gives us such peace to know we are exactly where the Lord wants us to be. And though the work is not completed, the house is now a home. It reminds us so much of ourselves and how the Lord is perfecting us; seeing us not as we are, but as we shall be. Even when we can't see, we can still trust that He is preparing us for an eternal future with Him.

This event in our lives is what we now refer to as our "Red Sea" experience because it strengthened our faith and trust in the One who knows our every need and has made provision for us. He clearly displayed His love for us. We praise Him to this day for all He has done, is doing, and will continue to do as we remain faithful. We are sure that this story won't be complete until the Lord comes. Many more exciting miracles and surprises are still taking place! I can't wait to see Him and the place He has prepared for us in His city! What unspeakable joy and blessing that will be!

As we wrap up this chapter of our story, let me share the tying of the bow on the Lord's great gift. Three months after we moved into our new house just outside the little town of Mathias, we attended Jere and Linda Franklin's workshop, "You Can Survive," in New Jersey. For the first time, in a public setting, we shared our Red Sea experience; how the Lord had led us to our beautiful acreage while we were without a job, and with very little money.

"Do you know what the word *Mathias* means?" Linda asked us after the meeting.

We shook our heads. She opened her Bible and pointed to the definition of the word.

"It means 'Gift of Jehovah.'"

Personal Comments

In the book *Maranatha*, we read about Adam being reinstated to his garden home and being *…transported with joy, he beholds the trees that were once his delight—the very trees whose fruit he himself had gathered in the days of his innocence and joy. He sees the vines that his own hands have trained, the very flowers that he once loved to care for. His mind grasps the reality of the scene; he comprehends that this is indeed Eden restored* (page 354).

Stanley is convinced that, in a similar way, Jesus will bring us back to this mountain in the earth made new and we, as Adam, with joy inexpressible, will recognize our "Eden home." Then, as promised in Isaiah, we shall build our house here and dwell in it and we shall plant vineyards and eat the fruit of them. We will call it *Mathias* even then, because we believe this is Jehovah's gift to us not only for this life, but all eternity.

We leave you with the promise that we claimed through our Exodus experience to the country, Jeremiah 29:11. *I know the plans I have for you saith the Lord, plans to prosper you and not to harm you, plans to give you hope and a future.* If God has placed on your heart the desire to "escape" to the country, *Be still and know that He is God* (Psalm 46:10).

The scriptures are full of promises about God's leading and guiding. Find the ones that speak to you and claim them. "Jehovah's gift" for you has already been orchestrated, but you will never find it unless you allow Him to lead. *Our heavenly Father has a thousand ways to provide for us, of which we know nothing. Those who accept the one principle of making the service and honor of God supreme will find perplexities vanish, and a plain path before their feet* (*The Desire of Ages*, p. 330).

God wants to work mightily in your life. Place your trust fully in Him. Make the service and honor of God supreme and He will lead you to the special place reserved for you.

We hope you have been encouraged by hearing about "Jehovah's gift" to us. We know you will enjoy His gift to you even more! God bless you in your journey.

————————

Dear readers, Piper recently passed away after bravely battling cancer for a short time. Her faith increased in proportion to the weakening of her body. Stanley was by her side, faithfully caring for her every need, enjoying her company, encouraging her spiritually, right to her last breath. In her last days, Stanley captured her beautifully uplifting story on a music CD he has entitled "The Caged Bird Set Free". It is a great witnessing tool to those who are struggling with cancer, past regrets, or need an uplift from the valley of discouragement.

To order their CD, contact Stanley via e-mail: ivinsimprovements@gmail.com

"Get Ready, Get Ready, Get Ready!"

DAVID LEHRMAN

And he shall go before him in the spirit and power of Elias,
to turn the hearts of the fathers to the children,
and the disobedient to the wisdom of the just;
to make ready a people prepared for the Lord.
Luke 1:17

It was the last day of our seminar at Garden State Academy in Tranquility, New Jersey. Jeanne sidled shyly over to where I (Linda) was selling copies of my husband's, book, **You Can Survive!** *She told me that she was at our seminar because of a series of strange and unlikely events. With tears in her eyes she assured me, "Now I know why I was directed to this place!" As she shared her story, I sensed, again, the importance that heaven places upon leaving the cities in preparation for the tough times to come. Here, David tells their story.*

Pennsylvania has always been home to Jeanne and me. When we were baptized in March of 2001, we became focused on finding and following present truth. Little did we know then that our journey would lead us far from our roots, but we are so thankful for the roots we discovered!

In the fall of 2004 Jeanne and I were planning our vacation for the next year. We scheduled a week in October with no apparent reason in mind, for we had never taken a week in October prior to that year. That spring, on three occasions over a period of many weeks, Jeanne, in her private personal evening devotions, received a distinct impression, though not in an audible voice, "GET READY, GET READY, GET READY!" The good Lord was working and we knew it not!

That summer, our friend, Jose, from Lafayette, NJ, sent us a book entitled *You Can Survive!*, by Jere Franklin. He also forwarded us an invitation to attend a week long seminar hosted by Jere, Linda, and Jed Franklin, now the very week we had chosen for vacation in October! Providence, we believe.

We learned many things that week and made many new friends. Because of that seminar, the desire to live in the country was awakened in our hearts. We knew that we must make a move because we believe the Bible and the Spirit of Prophecy. We had so much "stuff" after being married 12 years that we felt a need to simplify. We got a computer in order to sell things on e-Bay. What a good response we had! With that money in hand, we began an earnest search for property but couldn't find a piece with the three requirements needed: agricultural land, timber, and water.

Then we went to Hartland's spring camp meeting in 2006 where we met a man named Larry who had a friend in Tennessee with a property and house for sale with all the features we wanted. It was within our budget, so in July we went to see the property. We loved the area and the property and agreed to purchase this beautiful piece.

Highs and Lows

Jeanne retired that November and we finally got our house in Pennsylvania up for sale in February of '07. We signed an agreement in July with settlement in September of that year. During our home inspection

it was found that we had a water problem, among other things, and our prospective buyers got cold feet. We were worried that we would lose the deal on the Tennessee property, but the Lord helped us. In April of 2008 we had another agreement in place. Ten days before closing the deal, the man who was purchasing our buyer's property passed away. At this point our potential buyers wanted our property so badly that they offered to pay our taxes if we would take our house off the market! We agreed. They had another agreement in a few weeks so we, once more, had another settlement date. This time we had rented a twenty-six foot Penske truck and had it fully loaded the day before settlement. Then the settlement fell through!

My O my! Load. Unload. (By the way, we highly recommend Penske: they went above and beyond what we expected!) At this point my employer, of nearly nineteen years had already given me a "going away party," and I had set a quitting date three different times! I was perplexed and self conscious, as many of my coworkers suspected that I was being less than truthful. Our buyers speculated settlement for August 13, 2008. At this point I had no vacation days left, so I had to be at work. My employer had been very gracious already, so Jeanne went to the settlement hearing without me. When I called her from work and learned it was a done deal, I was so relieved! Praise God!

We have been here over five years, now, and the Lord has blessed in so many ways. Every Sunday we go to flea markets to hand out DVDs and witness for our faith. When our friends, John and Joan, came for a visit, they went to the flea market with us and met Randy, a man to whom we had been witnessing. John shared some sermon DVDs with Randy while another man, William, was at Randy's stand. William listened intently to the conversation between Randy and John. William was at the flea market searching for videos about the Bible. He had prayed the night before that God would send him truth. He had not yet been able to find a church home in his own town where he felt comfortable. He was happy to take the DVDs we offered. Would you believe it? He kept the very next Sabbath! Three months from that day, William was baptized!

We met new friends in the faith selling books at the flea market. I asked them if they would like to team up. Now, we are setting up every Sunday for the past several months, giving books to some who cannot afford to buy them. We have given out hundreds of DVDs. What a blessing! I have been able to make sales from my table for income, and our new friends are doing well on their book sales in addition to numerous witnessing opportunities!

Update

August 2012 marks four years that we've been out of city and off the grid. It is also our second anniversary as members of the Lincoln Memorial University organic gardening project, which has been very helpful with our gardening endeavors.

We just updated our solar system and what a blessing; four more solar panels with lots of extra power. There's so much with which the Lord keeps blessing us.

When we decided to move to the country, the funds we received from eBay sales really helped us with our moving expenses and reduced the amount of household goods we had to move. Little did I know, at the time, that I was in sales training for making extra money in our new location. We are now going to auctions, thrift stores, flea markets, and enjoy reselling the goods we buy. We set up every Sunday at the flea markets Jeanne has a booth at the indoor market while I set up at the outdoor market. We are learning to match items on eBay with those in demand at the flea market. It is interesting to see how this incorporates into an outreach ministry with customers that come to us.

Certainly the Lord has blessed us, for we have many success stories and a minimal amount of mistakes!

––––––––

Feel free to contact us 610-393-6536, or 610-393-6536, or dvd.lehrman@gmail.com

FOUR

Our Call To Leave

JOE COOPER

He that tilleth his land shall have plenty of bread.
Proverbs 28:19

*Joe and Teresa were already trying to discover an "escape route" when they attended one of our **You Can Survive!** weekend seminars in West Virginia. Shortly thereafter, they found their home in the country and have sent us pictures of their beautiful garden. Joe relates their "way of escape".*

On a 3×5 card, under the heading, "THIS IS WHY WE ARE GOING" we copied the following quotation in the summer of 2006.

In retired places, where we are farthest from the corrupting maxims, customs,

*and excitements of the world, and nearest to the heart of nature, Christ
makes His presence real to us, and speaks to our souls of His peace and love
(Fundamentals of Christian Education, page 424).*

We certainly were in great need of Christ's presence and peace. The
lifestyle we had been living, and the things for which were striving, had
become oppressive and meaningless. For several years, we both worked
two jobs. Joe's work was especially stressful, and he would often literally
run from appointment to appointment. We had a sense that it was crazy,
but we couldn't seem to see any way out. Mercifully, God has a hundred
ways to get our attention and open our eyes. Sometimes these eye-open-
ing experiences involve our health.

Joe began to suffer medical symptoms that led to the emergency room
of our local hospital, and before we had time to think, he was having
heart bypass surgery. This meant an enforced eight-week recovery period
away from work.

Shortly before this time, Teresa had quit her job to help Joe with his
work, so this meant we were both able to spend this time together in
reflection, talking, walking, and reading. We realized that God was calling us back to Him. We saw our nominal Christian experience for what
it really was. Our hearts longed for a more meaningful experience, not
only with our God, but also with each other. Thus began a journey that,
for us, was largely a quest for TIME—time for the things that matter
most——time for God, time for each other and time for others.

About that same time, we became aware of the ministry of Jim and
Sally Hohnberger and attended an *Empowered Living Ministries* camp
meeting. Everyone's experience is different, but we could certainly re-

late to what they shared. If you have not read the book, *Escape to God*, we would encourage you to do so. It had a profound impact on our lives. It was our first introduction to the importance of being in the country, away from the influences of the city, where we can more easily hear the voice of God. Since that time, our study of the Bible, the Spirit of Prophecy, and the work of other ministries, we have been lead to realize that country living is God's will for His people. It has *always* been His will!

Where did God place Adam and Eve in the beginning? In a garden! Through the Bible we see God's people choosing a rural lifestyle as opposed to the cities of their time. The children of Seth dwelt in the mountains so they could maintain a pure worship of God (*Patriarchs and Prophets*, page 81). Enoch placed himself and his family in the country, and from there he went forth to preach in the cities. Lot chose the luxury of the city, while Abraham was content to live a simple country life. Moses spent forty years in the mountains tending sheep, unlearning His city education and learning God's ways. Elijah lived *among the mountains… far removed from any city of renown* (*Prophets and Kings*, page 119). John the Baptist *lived in the quiet retreat of the wilderness… he chose the wilderness as his school, in which his mind could be properly educated and disciplined from God's great book of nature* (*Spirit of Prophecy*, vol. 2, page 46).

Reasons to Come Out

Jim Hohnberger lists eight compelling reasons to move away from the cities.

1) Spiritual prosperity

The most important reason for country living is to develop a deeper relationship with God and to develop a Christ-like character: *Character building is the most important work ever entrusted to human beings; and never before was its diligent study so important as now* (*Education*, page 225).

We are told that character building is *tenfold harder for both parents and children* in the cities (see *Fundamentals of Christian Education*, page 326). We both realize that we need all the help we can get to form characters in which the love of Jesus is lived out in our lives. This is the great need of all of God's people.

2) Protection from disasters

The time is near when the large cities will be visited by the judgments of God. In a little while, these cities will be terribly shaken (*Country Living*, page 7).

Are we seeing an indication of this in recent natural metropolitan calamities and the paralyzing fear of economic disaster showing itself in the worst way in densely populated areas?

3) Shield our families

There is not one family in a hundred who will be improved physically, mentally, or spiritually, by residing in the city. Faith, hope, love, happiness, can far better be gained in retired places, where there are fields and hills and trees (*Manuscript 76, 1905, Country Living*, page 13).

4) Health

It was not God's purpose that people should be crowded into cities, huddled together in terraces and tenements. In the beginning He placed our first parents amidst the beautiful sights and sounds He desires us to rejoice in today. The more nearly we come into harmony with God's original plan, the more favorable will be our position to secure health of body, and mind, and soul (Medical Ministry, pages 363-365).

Experts tell us that a deadly flu pandemic is likely in the near future, and the congestion of the cities will promote the rapid spread of pestilences, whatever form they take. Municipal water supplies are not pure. They come from impure sources and are treated with chemicals. In addition, they are infused with a myriad of prescription medications that are flushed into them. For us, one of the most important criteria in searching for our country property would be pure water. In the country, a person can more easily obtain all of God's eight natural remedies for maintaining and/or regaining health—including fresh air, pure water, sunshine, wholesome exercise, simple food grown organically in healthy soil, and better rest: *The sleep of a labouring man is sweet,* (Ecclesiastes 5:12). What joy to learn to trust more fully in God!

5) Freedom of worship and liberty of conscience

The Sunday party is strengthening itself in its false claims, and this will mean oppression to those who determine to keep the Sabbath of the Lord. We are to place ourselves where we can carry out the Sabbath commandment in its fullness. "Six days shalt thou labor," the Lord declares, "and do all thy work; but the seventh day is the Sabbath of the Lord thy God: in it thou shalt not do any work." And we are to be careful not to place ourselves where it will be hard for ourselves and our children to keep the Sabbath (Country Living, page 20).

6) Time will come when we can't buy and sell

Again and again the Lord has instructed that our people are to take their families away from the cities, into the country, where they can raise their own provisions; for in the future the problem of buying and selling will be a very serious one (Adventist Home, page 141).

We see a parallel between putting ourselves in the best position possible to remain faithful during the time when we cannot buy or sell, and putting ourselves in the best position today in all other areas of life in order to remain faithful to God and avoid sin. Surely, with the current economic crisis throughout the whole world, we are experiencing just a taste of what it could be like when all of our financial resources are cut off.

7) Raise our own provisions

He that tilleth his land shall have plenty of bread: but he that followeth after vain persons shall have poverty enough (Proverbs 28:19).

I see the necessity of the people of God moving out of the cities into retired country [places,] where they may cultivate the land and raise their own produce. Thus they may bring their children up with simple, healthful habits. I see the necessity of making haste to get all things ready for the crisis (Letter 90, 1897, *Country Living*, page 21).

Even secular people are realizing that raising food makes sense. It is more economical, much more nutritious and tasty, and provides good exercise in the fresh air and sunshine. Someone has said, "The best health insurance is served at the table."

8) Educate the children

Out of the cities is my message for the education of our children (*Country Living*, page 13).

In addition to the eight reasons listed above, country living makes it easier to free ourselves from the things and ways of the world. In the country, our minds are not continually assaulted with Satan's commercial entrapments.

The story is told of an ammunition factory in Panama during WWII. Authorities tried repeatedly over a period of time to get the Panama workers to work overtime, promising them good overtime pay. The people consistently refused, saying they did not need more money because they already had enough to meet all their needs. Finally, someone came up with an idea. A Sears and Roebuck catalog was sent to the home of every worker. When the people started looking through those catalogs, they discovered all kinds of things they didn't know they needed, and they began working the requested overtime.

Moving Forward

"Overcoming inertia," says our new friend Jere Franklin, "is the hardest part of the decision to move to the country."

I could not sleep past two o'clock this morning. During the night season I was in council. I was pleading with some families to avail themselves of God's appointed means, and get away from the cities to save their children. Some were loitering, making no determined efforts. The angels of mercy hurried Lot and his wife and daughters by taking hold of their hands. Had Lot hastened as the Lord desired him to, his wife would not have become a pillar of salt. Lot had too much of a **lingering spirit**. *Let us not be like him. The same voice that warned Lot to leave Sodom bids us, "Come out from among them, and be ye separate,… and touch not the unclean." Those who obey this warning will find a refuge. Let every man be wide awake for himself, and try to save his family. Let him gird himself for the work. God will reveal from point to point what to do next (Review and Herald, December 11, 1900).*

David Gates relates a recent study revealing three types of people in any emergency situation: five to ten percent of them become hysterical, seventy to eighty percent just freeze in place, with only five to ten percent will be able to act (either to save themselves or others). He inspired me to be among those who act. Everyone's situation is different, but we have discovered that God leads as we to follow His directions, step by step. There will be those who cannot make this move to the country "on their own" and will need to team up with others. Some may need to make changes in employment to allow them to move to the country. By letting the principles of God's Word, and the promptings of the Holy Spirit be our guide, we will not fail of success.

Now that we realize it is not God's purpose that we should live in the cities, and we understand some of the reasons, where do we start? Our personal instruction from God came through to us loud and clear, and was threefold:

- ◆ Simplify our lives
- ◆ Get out of debt
- ◆ Move to a quiet country location

It was also very clear that each facet of this plan can, and must, begin now, right where we were.

Simplifying Our Lives

We started selling or giving away all the unnecessary "stuff" we had so foolishly accumulated. Jere refers to "stuff", in his **You Can Survive!** seminars, as "the eighth plague." If it doesn't serve a useful purpose, it's a liability. Clutter robs us of peacefulness and consumes the precious resource of TIME. Do we really need all those magazines, clothes, dishes, toys, etc.? What about our activities? Are we spending too much time in front of the TV or computer? We discovered that we needed to give up some of the "good" things we were doing in order to have time for the "best."

Getting Out of Debt

Our mortgage was our main debt. We asked ourselves, "Can we make mortgage payments during the time when God's people cannot buy or sell?" Our research turned up some key texts.

When one becomes involved in debt, he is in one of Satan's nets, which he sets for souls (*Adventist Home*, page 392).

The borrower is servant to the lender (Proverbs 22:7). When we are in debt, we are slaves to a payment plan. It causes an unquiet spirit, and, in the near future, indebtedness will become even more enslaving.

Abstracting and using money for any purpose, before it is earned, is a snare (*Adventist Home*, page 392).

We went to work doing all we could to relieve our debt while claiming His promise: *If we ask any thing according to his will, he heareth us; and if we know that he hear us, whatsoever we ask, we know that we have the petitions that we desired of him* (I John 5:14-15).

It was time to sell our place.

Move to a Quiet Country Location

After we were convinced that God wanted us to make a move, we felt directed to a certain area of the country. We started researching for a church family that had our same view of God's love and interest in witnessing for our Savior that we had. After we found our church home, we obtained a map of the county and started driving up and down the roads. As we drove the roads, we colored them in on the map and made notes of things we wanted to remember. Whenever we saw someone in their yard or sitting on their porch, we would stop and talk with them, inquiring if they knew of any land for sale.

We also worked with a realtor, but we didn't find the property through the realtor! We would eventually find our property by following one lead after another. Some of the people we met during our searching time have become precious friends, and we still visit them. We have had opportunities to share our testimony and pray with them.

The Property

What should we look for in a country property? There are three basic needs—water, soil suitable for growing food, and wood. We recommend developing two lists– a basics list and a wish list. For us, our combined wish/basics list included: privacy, five to ten acres with a good garden area, woods, affordable, stream, easy access, and should be within thirty minutes of church.

Water is one of our most basic needs. Think about having to access water without electrical power. A spring is ideal. Wells can also be made accessible with a specialized hand pump, if they are not too deep.

It is necessary to have a source of wood for cooking and heating.

The property must include terrain and soil that is suitable for growing fruits and vegetables. *Prepare thy work without, and make it fit for thyself in the field, and afterwards build thine house* (Proverbs 24:27). One of the first things we did with our property was to plant fruit trees, berry bushes, and asparagus. Then we started developing the garden area.

It is important to obtain a septic permit before you purchase the property. Make sure the purchase agreement is contingent on septic approval. Insure there are no easements. Check on possible zoning issues, flood plain issues, deed restrictions, and that you will have clear mineral and timber rights for the property.

Finally, we vowed not to bring the city with us! We seriously considered our basic needs, and simplified our life style to minimize distractions. It was a cleansing experience to determine our basic needs and then rid ourselves of the fluff.

Stages of a Vision

We advise folks not to become discouraged if their plans don't happen as quickly as they would like. After we began looking for property, it was ten months before we made a purchase. Then our move was delayed for almost two years more while we tried to sell the house in which we were living. It was an opportunity to wait upon the Lord and learn to trust His perfect timing and faithfulness. *All things do work together for the good of those who love Him* (Romans 8:28).

During this time, it was helpful to understand the three stages of a vision. First, the vision is born. Second, the vision dies. Third, the vision is realized. For example, Moses had the vision of delivering his people from the oppression of Egypt. Using his own wisdom he took things into his own hands and the result was that he had to flee for his life, and his vision died. For 40 years he lived with the death of his vision; however, this was the most important time of his life. God was retraining Moses in His school. Many of God's people are in this training period now. God in His great mercy has given us this preparation time.

It's About Obedience

God did not call us to country living to be "hermits." He called us to be HIS! Country living is about obedience (God has *told* us to go!). It's about character development. He says, *Be ye holy, even as I am holy* (I Peter 1:16). It's about learning self-denial, learning to live the life of total surrender to and dependence upon God. It's about helping others. For us, we needed to begin right where we were, before we moved to the country.

We have a friend who started a garden in her backyard in the city because she heard God's voice telling her to grow her own food. Another friend lives in a condominium with very limited space, but has found a couple of places to grow vegetables. Everyone can grow sprouts, which are among the most nutritious of foods. We need good nutrition in order to arise and shine for God in these last days. So, until we are able to leave the city, we can all take steps to do whatever we can to be obedient, and God will bless. If we are obedient to the light we have at each step, then God will lead us to the next step.

Whatever the situation, obedience to what God shows us ensures His presence and His blessing. This is what we all want.

If ye be willing and obedient, ye shall eat the good of the land (Isaiah 1:19).

Trust in the Lord, and do good; so shalt thou dwell in the land, and verily thou shalt be fed. Delight thyself also in the Lord, and he shall give thee the desires of thine heart. Commit thy way unto the Lord; trust also in him, and he shall bring it to pass (Psalm 37:3-5).

Final Thoughts

The horse is prepared against the day of battle; but safety is of the Lord (Proverbs 21:31).

Lessons we are learning: 1) self-distrustfulness—we have made many mistakes relying on our own wisdom, 2) faith and trust, 3) death to self, and 4) waiting upon the Lord. *Faithful is He who called us, and HE will do it* (I Thessalonians 5:24).

Let there be nothing done in a disorderly manner, that there shall be a great loss or sacrifice made upon property because of ardent, impulsive speeches which stir up an enthusiasm which is not after the order of God, that a victory that was essential to be gained, shall, for lack of levelheaded moderation and proper contemplation and sound principles and purposes, be turned into a defeat. Let there be wise generalship in this matter, and all move under the guidance of a wise, unseen Counselor, which is God. Elements that are human will struggle for the mastery, and there may be a work done that does not bear the signature of God. Now I plead with every soul to look not too strongly and confidently to human counselors, but look most earnestly to God, the one wise in counsel. Submit all your ways and your will to God's ways and to God's will... (Country Living, p. 27)

God is teaching us how to better use the precious talent of time. In His mercy, He has promised to redeem the time we have selfishly and foolishly wasted. We are attempting to order our lives so that we always have time for others whenever opportunities present themselves.

Gaining a deeper experience with Jesus is the most precious part of our journey to the country. We pray this will be your experience too. It is our earnest prayer that we may all say in that day very soon, *Lo, this is our God; we have waited for Him and He will save us. This is the Lord; we have waited for Him; we will be glad and rejoice in His salvation* (Isaiah 25:9).

Books that have been especially helpful to us:

Biblical Response Therapy, by Daniel Gabbert

Country Living, by Ellen White

Escape to God, by Jim Hohnberger

From City to Country Living, by Arthur L. White and E. A. Sutherland

His Robe or Mine, by Frank Phillips

You Can Survive, by Jere Franklin

Helpful Web sites for Country Living:

http://www.bereagardens.org

http://countrylivinguniversity.com

http://ths.gardenweb.com

http://www.growministries.net

Http://www.mountainmediaministries.com

http://www.youcansurvive.org

Web sites for Spiritual Growth:

http://www.audioverse.org

http://www.justifiedwalk.com

http://www.youcansurvive.org

FIVE

Roots in Our Blood

ELLIOTT TAM

Trust in the LORD with all thine heart
and lean not unto thine own understanding.
In all thy ways acknowledge him, and he shall direct thy paths.
Proverbs 3:5, 6

Elliott Tam holds the distinction of being the first person in Canada to order a Closing Events Chart from us! The Tam Family's "escape" was e-mailed to us before we met them in person, in August of 2008, when Elliott, Heather, and their two children, came to our Family Camp. They have been an encouragement to us, and we are sure that you will enjoy getting to know them, too, through their story, as told by Elliott.

Elliott writes: *Hi Jere! Thanks for your book,* **You Can Survive!** *Since I last talked with you on the phone, God has opened the way for me to move away from the city. Your book has been a real blessing and encouragement to me and my family as we prayed about our big move! Please find our testimony attached. Hope the miracles that God has done will also be an encouragement as you continue doing His will. Take care and hope to meet you some day as I'd like to tell you, in person, about how God has led us over the last twelve months in our move to the country!*

January

Opening an *Amazing Facts* catalog, I stumble across a book entitled *You Can Survive!,* by Jere Franklin. It talks about how to prepare for moving to the country. It catches my eye, so I order it. For the month of January, I read it on the bus to and from work. I also read again E. G. White's booklet, *Country Living*. I discover exciting quotes:

"Better than any other inheritance of wealth you can give to your children will be the gift of a healthy body, a sound mind, and a noble character. Those who understand what constitutes life's true success will be wise betimes. They will keep in view life's best things in their choice of a home. Instead of dwelling where only the works of men can be seen, where the sights and sounds frequently suggest thoughts of evil, where turmoil and confusion bring weariness and disquietude, go where you can look upon the works of God. Find rest of spirit in the beauty and quietude and peace of nature. Let the eye rest on the green fields, the groves, and the hills. Look up to the blue sky, unobscured by the city's dust and smoke, and breathe the invigorating air of heaven. Go where, apart from the distractions and dissipations of city life, you can give your children your companionship, where you can teach them to learn of God through His works, and train them for lives of integrity and usefulness" (The Ministry of Healing, pp. 265-267).

"He [Enoch] *did not make his abode with the wicked. He did not locate in Sodom, thinking to save Sodom. He placed himself and his family where the atmosphere would be as pure as possible. Then at times, he went forth to the inhabitants of the world with his God-given message"* (*The Seventh Day Adventist Bible Commentary*, EGW Comments, vol. 1, p. 1087).

I look up to see myself surrounded by the city. I share my convictions with Heather. We discuss what to do. As we study together, two goals become clear:

1) to serve God in ministry: people need to know Jesus in small towns as well as large cities and we decide that we do not want to minister while living in a large city, and

2) to raise our children in the best environment to learn about God. Living in Langley, BC, we notice the negative effects on our children—malls, crowding, lack of natural surroundings for teaching them about God.

February

For the last couple of years, we've been thinking of home schooling our children. Mariah will be starting kindergarten in September and we realize that it's a HUGE burden for Heather alone to take care of both children, look after the home, and teach home school. I know that I need to be home more to help train the kids spiritually, as well as relieve Heather so she can have more time to put into home schooling.

March

We call a realtor to find out what we can sell our home for. In preparation for our move to the country, we plant a larger garden and two fruit trees (unfortunately, no fruit until next year).

Two months have gone by and I am feeling discouraged because there are no British Columbia Hydro (BCH) jobs on the bulletin boards suitable for me to get transferred. My background, an electrical engineer, has given me employment at BCH for thirteen years. It is an excellent company with great pay, good benefits, and eight weeks of vacation time! I thought that God would give me a job in a more rural location and that I should be transferred by now.

In my discouragement, Pastor Ray just happened to have the perfect sermon for me that Sabbath. He felt called to be a pastor many years ago and started studying at Canadian Union College, but halfway

through his course, someone discouraged him from becoming a pastor, so he went back to logging. Twelve years later, he felt called again. This time he finished his pastoral studies, and became an evangelist for the BC Conference. He said that he regretted not finishing the first time and lost twelve years of being an evangelist, a work which he enjoyed tremendously. He encouraged me to stick with my convictions.

Heather's dad is a very spiritual man whom I greatly respect. Three years ago, when we talked with him about moving to the country, we could tell that he was concerned because Heather was pregnant with Caleb at the time. Perhaps the world circumstances were not as bad as today. Then, in March when we mentioned that we felt called to move, he agreed that "now is the time". Caleb is older and the world is so much worse: terrorism, natural disasters, and other signs of the end. We need to finish God's work!

God always gave me special Bible texts as well. One of my favorites has always been Proverbs 3:5, 6: "*Trust in the LORD with all your heart and lean not on your own understanding; in all your ways acknowledge him, and he shall direct your paths*" (NKJV).

April

Since no engineering jobs are opening up for me at BCH, I start knocking on other doors. One prayer that I keep asking God to answer is for Him to close all the doors that I knock on EXCEPT the one which He wants me to go through. I apply to other companies that hire engineers such as *Aquila* (similar to BCH but they supply power to the Okanagan and the Kootenay areas), and *Amec Mining*. I put my name in to *Job Finders*, a company that matches employee skills with employers' needs. I discover that there are three jobs for which I qualify, even without an interview: one is in the US, the second one is in the province of New Brunswick, and the third one is in Trail, BC. God is answering my prayer! The most likely job is in Trail. (Several months later, when we drove through Trail, we had more than one reason to be thankful that God did not move us there!) We want to stay in Canada, preferably British Columbia, or New Brunswick, where Heather's parents reside.

We discover that I cannot work in NB because I am not bilingual (don't speak French). Moving to the USA is not an option because we want our parents to be able to move close to us (they are not US citizens). In the end, none of the jobs available seem to fit.

A friend e-mails me information on an organic asparagus farm in Grand Forks but the problem is that we can't survive on the wage offered, and we are worried about what to do with two-thousand pounds of asparagus if we cannot sell it!

Instead of despairing, I choose to claim a promise: *For with God nothing shall be impossible.* Luke 1:37

May

Culligan Water has a district person in the East and West Kootenays. Talking with him on the phone, he says he is willing to split his territory, giving half to me because he is too busy. That sounds good to me! My hopes rise, but he never calls back. God closed that door.

Our first choice for the location of a home most suitable for us (I seem to recall a Spirit of Prophecy reference about choosing a suitable home location, but am unable to find it when I search) is Creston, BC for four reasons:

1) Ed, Heather's brother, lives in Creston and he is a tremendous resource when it comes to gardening, outdoor life skills, etc.

2) Residents say the weather is perfect—not too cold and not too hot, good climate for having a garden.

3) It is beautiful valley, very scenic.

4) A nice church with over a hundred people attending each Sabbath. There is also a church school. If we move there, Heather is hoping that her parents will move there instead of living so far away. They have told us that they like the small town environment they find in Creston.

June

I see that *Creston Auto Glass* is for sale. When I inquire, the realtor says it is a profitable business. My only concern is my back; I cannot lift anything too heavy. Plus, if a store window got broken on Friday night, they may need service, and I do not want to work evenings or Sabbaths.

I discover that BCH has some job openings in small towns, but they are managerial positions which would, more than likely, require travel to the lower mainland, and work on Sabbath and evenings when equipment breaks down or during yearly maintenance. As Heather and I discuss each job, we know that God does not want us to take these positions as it would mean the same amount of time I am currently spending away from home, or maybe even more time.

July

Friends tell us that in Trail, the real estate is some of the cheapest available in all of Canada. We phone a realtor and he says he will send us info, but we never hear from him. In fact, two different realtors promise to send us information but fail to do so. We decide God does not want us to go there! Seven months have passed since I first attempted to change jobs, and we realize that if God wants me to spend more time with my family and training the children, then we need a miracle! We ask for one.

"Dear Father, you know our hearts. We want to follow your counsel and move to the country. We have prayed that You will close all the doors except the one that You want us to go through. It has been six months and we have knocked on many doors. Please show us where we should locate and what job to look for. We claim Your promise in Matthew 6:33: *Seek ye first the kingdom of God and His righteousness and all these things shall be added unto you.*"

August

At camp meeting in Hope, BC, we ask everyone we meet, "Are you from Creston?"

On August 20, the realtor in Creston tells me that *Pace Setter Developers* is planning to build a new seniors apartment in Creston. I think to myself that they may want to hire a manager or maintenance person. I look them up on the Internet and discover that they are linked to *Golden Life Management*. I feel discouraged because this sounds like two big companies that work together and that I will have a difficult time getting in, but then I remember that I have knocked on so many doors already that one more won't hurt! Whatever the answer, God is still in control. With a prayer in my heart, I phone Endre, the developer, and find out that he IS looking for a manager! The next day, the phone rings. It's Endre.

"Elliott," Endre assures me, "since you have an engineering background, you may also qualify for two other positions here: construction coordinator, and site supervisor."

In the course of the conversation, I tell him that I want Sabbaths off and that I only want to work thirty hours per week. The thirty hour restriction is difficult. Who wants to hire someone on a part time basis? Yet, I feel convicted that working full time will not allow me to help with home schooling, plus maintain a garden, and spend the kind of family time that we believe Jesus wants us to have. Heather keeps insisting that we need to put family first and to trust God. Well, Endre assures me that having Sabbaths off and working only thirty hours a week will not be a problem, unless I am to take the site supervisory position. We are excited and start packing for the interview! We hope to leave September 6 (last day of the Labor Day, the long weekend).

Tuesday, September 7

We drive through Castlegar on the way to Creston, and stop by one of the senior apartments that *Pace Setter* has developed. We want to talk with the manager who has the same position that I desire to have in Creston. She tells me that the first year, she worked long hours and had to hire and fire staff.

"If the dishwasher did not show up," she says with a shake of her head, "I had to stay and finish the dishes!" She explained that she had about forty staff members and seventy senior rooms. After the meeting, I feel discouraged. The hours are too long. Is God calling us to move to the country at the sacrifice of our family time? Not likely, since that is part of the reason we are moving in the first place. This is the first time that we have felt the call to step through a door, but now it seems like it's closing. Should we go home?

I keep singing the Bible verse to myself, *"Trust in the Lord with all of your heart, and lean not on your own understanding, in all your ways acknowledge Him, and He shall direct your paths"* (Proverbs 3:5, 6).

Wednesday, September 8

We decide to meet Endre in Cranbrook, knowing that we should explore the construction coordinator position. During the drive, we reevaluate our priorities. Do we want to move to Creston because of Heather's parents, and Ed her brother (family), the big church and church school, the climate and scenery? The thought comes to us; maybe we should establish God and His work as our first priority and put our family in second place?

We remind each other that a speaker at camp meeting, Dr. Morris, sang a scripture song combining the words from Luke 10:2 and John 4:35; *"The harvest truly is great, but the laborers are few; therefore pray the Lord of the harvest to send out laborers into His harvest. Do you not say, There are still four months and then comes the harvest? Behold, I say to you, lift up your eyes and look at the fields, for they are already white for harvest!"*

That song, coupled with how God had been leading us to put Him first in everything, enables us to decide that God may want us in Cranbrook to help in the smaller church. The job may be better suited to my skills, as well, and less work hours required.

Ed, Heather's brother, tells us to check out a rural area along Ha Ha Creek road, so we take a drive out the rural road, fifteen minutes out of town. The scenery is amazingly beautiful! Ha Ha Creek road is an eighteen minute drive, and during that drive we see a family of turkeys, four small lakes, mountains on either side of the narrow valley (all agricultural land), neighbors not too far away, yet plenty of elbow room. It is so *beautiful!* My thoughts of Cranbrook are slowly changing.

Thursday, September 9

I meet Endre for the interview. As he describes the job, I begin to realize that it is perfect for me. The hours are flexible, I have Sabbaths off, and there will be opportunities to even work from my home computer at times. The only problem I can see is the pay: I will only make about half of my usual income, however, so I am VERY stressed. Discussing our budget with some friends, Heather and I are encouraged. Learning to be careful with money will certainly be a lifestyle change, but we are convinced that we can do it!

Friday, September 10

I accept the job in Cranbrook, but am still stressed about how much we will have to "cut corners". I remember walking into the grocery store and thinking about that. As I walk down the produce aisle, from which an ever-increasing percentage of our purchases are made, I realize that by growing a garden, we can decrease our food budget considerably.

"Ahmed," I told my BCH manager the next morning, "I'm quitting."

It is the end of an era. BCH was my employer for thirteen years. It's hard to believe that I'm quitting such a secure, high paying job. But if that's what God wants, then I'll do it. He will take care of our needs if we seek Him first. *Seek ye first the kingdom of God and His righteousness, and all these things* [food and clothing] *shall be added unto you* (Matthew 6:33).

I look forward every week to Friday night for Sabbath rest, but this week has been so stressful that I really do appreciate turning my brain "off" and enjoying peace and rest with Jesus and my family.

Saturday, September 11

We visit the Cranbrook church. It happens to be potluck so we meet many nice people. It is a very small congregation (twenty) and we are assured that God wants us here to help with music (they do not have a pianist, Heather's talent) and children's Sabbath school, maybe even some preaching because the pastor spends half of his time in Cranbrook and half in Creston.

After sundown I feel the financial stress returning. I phone two good friends that make about the same wage as I will be making in our new single income level.

"No problem, Elliott!" they assure me. "You can do it! God will help you!"

God, in the voice of a friend's reassurance, is encouraging me to accept the move. I find peace.

Sunday, September 12

Heather, has been telling me during this past week to pray more and work less, so I make sure that I have a nice, long season of personal devotions before starting my day. Every day feels like the first day of the rest of my life!

Today is the only day we have to look for a place to stay in Cranbrook. Everyone is advising us to rent for awhile to become familiar with the area before buying something. I look through the paper and find that there is only one mobile home in the country to rent. Unfortunately, it is already rented when I phone. All the other rental units are in town, which we did not want. Renting is challenging; if we wait until we arrive in Cranbrook in November, it will be winter and we will have to drive around hoping to find suitable rental units, plus we will also have to find someplace to store our stuff. Maybe God wants us to buy a place.

A few days ago, a realtor had printed all the MLS listings for me so, with that list in hand, we start driving. We look at the ten homes that are in our price range and within a fifteen minute radius of work. If possible, we do not want a mortgage and want to be debt free, according to numerous counsels in the Spirit of Prophecy. Plus, I feel more comfortable being debt-free with my reduced income. Unfortunately, none of the homes are suitable; they are either close to train tracks, freeways, or neighbors. We look at buying land without a house on it, but land is not cheap.

We really like Ha Ha Creek area but there is nothing for sale on MLS in that area. I phone Kathleen (a new acquaintance from church) who lives in the Ha Ha Creek area to ask if she knows anyone there who might be selling a home or property. She gives me three names. I phone the first person and they have thirty-one acres of farm land for $280,000. That is too expensive for us. The second person tells me that fifteen minutes further up the road, a developer is selling land. When I phone him, I discover that one acre will cost $100,000. I would have to build a log home or cedar home (log/cedar homes are expensive and high maintenance). The third person, Lawrence, is not home. I phone him many times during the day. No answer.

I go to an Internet café and find a private log home for sale. We go to see it thinking that maybe God wants us to reconsider a log home. We check it out and find that the walls (logs) need to be vacuumed often as well as the floor and that it would quadruple our cleaning requirements. But they do have a newer wood stove and it does not bother Heather (in the past, she has had an allergy to wood smoke.) We believe God wants us to visit the log home for two reasons:

1) We need to find out that a high efficiency wood stove is OK for Heather so we can go ahead and buy one to save money plus be prepared for the "end times" when we can't buy or sell.

2) We need to realize that we shouldn't buy any log home or consider the one acre property that requires us to build a log/cedar home.

I phone another realtor and tell her that we want a home that is fifteen minutes outside of town in the country and she says, "Everyone's looking for that...it's the hottest item. That's why there's nothing for sale!"

"We desperately need a miracle!" I tell Heather at supper time. I have a job but no place to live! During supper, the phone rings. It's Lawrence, the person I've been trying to call all day! (It is miraculous that he called us, because I didn't leave my name or phone number, and even if he had caller ID on his phone, it would only show the Motel name and not the room number where we are staying! I explain to him that we are looking for a home or property and he said that he could sell me a piece of land with a well on it already (having a pre-drilled well gives me great relief because, sometimes, digging a well can be VERY expensive especially if water is very deep underground). After supper, we drive there as fast as we can!

Ha Ha Creek road is an eighteen minute drive from end to end.

Lawrence's property is in the most beautiful stretch of this road with two lakes in front, a mountain in the back, and is located on the north side (sunnier side so less snow). He tells me that he is willing to sell me eight acres with a well for $110,000! Three acres of it is a field with rich top soil three feet deep, and five acres is up the mountain with trees for firewood! We are so excited. Is God opening the way? We decide to buy this piece of land!

Monday, September 13

The job in Cranbrook is just right for me. The owner says that he will try to get me some engineering work and pay me more for that work which will help us financially, too!

Heather, in the meantime, goes to Eagle Homes (modular home dealer) down the block to check out a single and double wide. She is happy with a double wide unit and the price is within our range, too!

In the afternoon, we start ordering the home and choosing the custom options. That is the fastest we've ever chosen paint colors, flooring, curtains and etc. It's like a game show where you are asked a question and have to answer as fast as possible! In a matter of hours, we have chosen what we want in our new home. They tell us they can build this home in six to eight weeks—just in time for my new job.

The only problem is that Lawrence wants $10 K deposit, and Eagle Homes wants $20 K deposit, and I do not have any money! I was not expecting to buy anything so fast! In addition, I also need a septic tank, electrical service, a water line to the well, and lots of permits (building, road, septic, etc.). I need my own project manager to help *me* because I am not even in Cranbrook yet!

That afternoon we pray for God to do miracles again. I am impressed to ask Lawrence, my new neighbor, if he will be willing to be the project manager and he says "Sure"! What an ideal setup! He is right there to oversee the project plus he says he can get permits, etc. That evening, I also find a contractor to dig up the land for the home pad, put in a septic field, and build a road!

Tuesday, September 14

Today we go to the notary public to sign the papers to purchase the land. Lawrence phones to say that he and his wife Bonnie discussed it and feels that we need to "trust each other," so he waives the $10K! Eagle Homes is willing to accept a VISA imprint and put our order in right away so we can have it in time for my new job! We are moving!

So, in five days, after making a commitment to what I knew to be God's will, Jesus gave me a job, eight acres of land, a modular home, and a project manager. And, would you believe, I did not even have to pay one cent!

Selling our Home

We tell the realtor about the Sabbath—that we do not want to do business after 4 PM Friday till sundown on Saturday (late in September sundown is getting earlier). The housing market is a little slow and there are many homes for sale in our neighborhood. We list our home for eight days and about ten people come through to view it. It is a bit stressful keeping everything tidy and stopping what we are doing to let them come!

After eight days, a serious offer comes through on Friday at noon. The realtor and other agents know we have only four hours to complete the deal. The buyer really likes our home and we accept the offer. It is only

$1500 less than the list price! The deal closes just after 4 PM—still well before sunset! What a beautiful Sabbath present; peace of mind that our house is sold. God has surely made a way for us.

Getting Settled

As we settle into our new home, God blesses us with our basic needs. We want to eat healthy food. When we decide to use *Silver Hills* bread, a sprouted grain loaf made by a BC bakery, God leads us to a discount store where they have a few loaves of *Silver Hills* bread, just waiting for us! We want to try ice skating on the lake nearby, but our daughter has no ice skates. We find a pair, just the right size, at a thrift store, for two dollars! We need to purchase books for home schooling. We discover that the church we now attend used to operate a church school downstairs so we have access to many of the very books we need, and we can use them whenever we want!

Small miracles, maybe, but they mean so much. We know that God is with us fulfilling His promises day by day. He led us here to our home in the country. And we love it!

We include outdoor work in our daily home school plans. Our son Caleb started working with me on outside projects and gardening when he was five years old. He is learning to look after his own garden plot. He plans what to plant in his portions of the greenhouse and our large garden. Elliott (Dad) works with Caleb and they do things together which makes it more enjoyable and bonding. Projects include gardening, changing oil (in the rototiller, lawnmowers, and other equipment), sharpening blades, repairing water lines, and setting up bird feeders and bird houses. Sometimes all four of us work outside together; when it's time to dig potatoes, and harvest other produce. Gardening teaches very valuable character traits: perseverance, attention to detail, and planning ahead. Our daughter, Mariah, doesn't enjoy gardening as much, but loves cooking, sewing, and music. In the winter, the children carry wood and chop kindling to help us all stay warm. It's a good way to take a productive fresh air break in the middle of Math class!

Summary Statements

"There is not one family in a hundred who will be improved physically, mentally, or spiritually, by residing in the city. Faith, hope, love, happiness, can far better be gained in retired places, where there are fields and hills and trees. Take your children away from the sights and sounds of the city, away from the rattle and din of streetcars and teams, and their minds will become more healthy. It will be found easier to bring home to their hearts the truth of the Word of God" (Country Living, page 13).

"The cities are to be worked from outposts. Said the messenger of God, Shall not the cities be warned? Yes; not by God's people living in them, but by their visiting them, to warn them of what is coming upon the earth" (Country Living, page 30).

"When iniquity abounds in a nation, there is always to be heard some voice giving warning and instruction, as the voice of Lot was heard in Sodom. Yet Lot could have preserved his family from many evils, had he not made his home in this wicked, polluted city. All that Lot and his family did in Sodom could have been done by them, even if they had lived in a place some distance away from the city. Enoch walked with God, and yet he did not live in the midst of any city, polluted with every kind of violence and wickedness, as did Lot in Sodom" (Evangelism, page 79).

Feller's Heights

LORETTA HOWARD

*Now unto Him that is able to do exceeding abundantly
above all that we ask or think…unto Him be the glory.*
Ephesians 3:20, 21
*And we know that all things work together for good
to them that love God, to them who are the called
according to His purpose.*
Romans 8:28
*…but he that putteth his trust in Me shall possess the land,
and shall inherit My holy mountain…*
Isaiah 57:13

*We have known Ellis and Loretta for many years. In the late 1970's, they
joined our staff at Sanctuary Ranch. We currently attend the same church
in Tumbler Ridge, BC. We are privileged to count them among our friends.
Loretta relates the basics of how they acquired their country property.*

1977-1997

Most of these years were given to the Lord working in supporting ministries assignments that paid only a stipend, so we had not amassed any wealth, not even a substantial savings account. We had not contributed any significant amount to Canada Pension Plan (CPP) toward our retirement years.

1997

We moved to Tumbler Ridge (TR), BC and Ellis began falling trees for a horse-logging operation during the winter months. Other income producing sources were running a green house, growing reclamation plants for the coal mine, farming (hay sales), firewood, and dog kennels.

Loretta was able to get various nursing jobs. In the fall of 1999, she began working part-time as Home and Community Nurse in Tumbler Ridge. Through these activities we began to become acquainted with many of the people who lived in Tumbler Ridge.

2001

Houses were selling very inexpensively in TR following the closing of the coal mines. Ellis had earlier approached representatives from the Canadian Mortgage and Housing Corporation (CMHC) about a particular house, but they weren't willing to negotiate at that time. When Dawson Creek Realty came into town to sell some of the mine houses, Ellis again contacted CMHC because the house we were looking at was not on the list for sale. At that time CMHC agreed to let the realtor sell the house to us. We were able to purchase (with a mortgage) for less than we had originally offered to CMHC (less than $35,000)! Our purpose in purchasing was so that we could have a place where our newly organized TR SDA Company could meet without renting a church or building.

We had chosen a corner lot in an easy-to-find location.

2003

Sanctuary Valley, a beautiful acreage just outside of Tumbler Ridge, where we had been living, was sold, so we moved into our house in TR.

2005

In the fall, our pastor, Rudy, spoke to us about a quarter-section of land

for sale along the Heritage Highway located about eighty kilometers from Tumbler Ridge and about thirty kilometers from Dawson Creek. Neither Ellis nor I could classify ourselves as "city-dwellers", and we had already been looking for an opportunity to purchase acreage outside of town, but nothing close to Tumbler Ridge was opening up. This property was close to power and had plenty of timber on it that could be used for firewood and building. Ellis walked through the property and found it to be an attractive country setting.

We weren't particularly excited about it because we felt that it was too far from Tumbler Ridge, no house, a questionable water source, and fronted the highway. We began praying about it believing that God knows all things, the end from the beginning, and that if this was His will He would make it plain to us. We weren't in a hurry, and it didn't really matter to either of us whether this would work out or not—we were still hoping for something closer to TR.

2006

In January we contacted the realtor and made a counteroffer, but the seller did not accept it, so we paid $1000 earnest money on the property. Our prayer was, "If God wants us to have this property, He can sell our house in time and for an amount that is adequate for us to accomplish what we need to do." Our agreement with the owner was on condition that we could sell our house and was effective until March 31. Several prospective buyers looked at our house right after we put it on the market, then no one came around for about six weeks! I was beginning to rejoice that I wouldn't have to move, but then another problem arose. At the end of January, I had retired because of employer policies. Without that income, how would we be able to make the mortgage payment?

About two weeks before the end of the agreement with the owner, another buyer came. They didn't waste any time negotiating and our house in TR was sold just in time! We moved out to the property in April and lived in our little camper while the building program progressed. The first structure to be built was a power shed so that we could be connected to electricity. Next, we built a structure we call our "summer kitchen." This is where we set up our wood cook stove. This enabled us to expand our living area beyond the cramped quarters of our camper.

In September our son, Jon, was married. Our daughter, Debbie, came up for the occasion. While she was here we walked out to the back of the property to show her around. Back there we are far enough from the highway so that not much traffic noise can be heard. At one point Debbie spotted an elk, but it was gone before she could call our attention to it! We have, since then, seen moose, deer, bear, and birds of many kinds. We also hear the coyotes howling from time to time.

Recounting Our Blessings

Our house in TR sold for enough money that we could pay cash for the acreage, be debt-free (including mortgage and vehicle payments) and be able to build a livable structure in time to move in before winter. We believe God lead in this purchase, and He continues to provide for us even in difficult times. We praise Him and give Him the honor.

At present, although our building program seems to have hit a speed bump, we never need to be worried about being bored with nothing to do! Living in the country, there is always something to "keep us young"!

We developed our garden site by pulling up some small poplar trees and hauling in topsoil. The neighbors have graciously offered us some composted manure which has enriched our site considerably. Our garden grows enough veggies to keep us right through the winter. I don't particularly care for home-canned veggies, so I either freeze or dry them. In the case of potatoes, our neighbors kindly lets us store them in a cool room at their house through the winter months. In return, they are welcome to use whatever they need. We have enjoyed getting acquainted with some of our neighbors, showing friendship, helping where and when we can—always praying and watching for the opportunity to share spiritual comfort and hope.

Since a major portion of our land is wooded, there is an adequate supply of firewood for heating. Ellis also bought a firewood permit from forestry to get firewood from the nearby "crown land" to sell or give to others as the opportunity indicates.

No matter what the season, there are always quiet walks to be taken, listening for the sounds of nature. Just last evening, walking from a wet area a short distance from the trail, we heard what, at first, sounded like ducks. Try as we might we could see no ducks. We finally concluded that it must be a froggy chorus! During the winter time, we have attempted cross-country skiing and snow-shoeing. (I am better with the latter!)

One winter we invited a group of friends from the Dawson Creek church and some other friends to come out to a bonfire to roast their 'veggie dogs,' and enjoy some good old-fashioned friendship.

The oil industry has become quite active in our area. They have arranged with us to construct a road along the south edge and across the back corner of our property to service one of their wells behind us. This gives us a small yearly income.

Even though we are nearer to the town of Dawson Creek, BC, we are still actively involved with the little church in Tumbler Ridge (one of the reasons for us moving there). The church in Tumbler started as a company in 1997. At first just a couple of families met at Sanctuary Valley where we were living at the time. As more people became involved, we rented another church in town for our Sabbath services. Then after buying the house in Tumbler we met there. About that time a number of Adventist families moved to Tumbler Ridge area and soon our house was too small! One of our members bought a commercial building in TR that had belonged to the Salvation Army. One end of the building had been renovated to be used for church services with a fellowship hall upstairs. As time progressed the Lord made it possible for us to "stratatize" the building so that the church could own its own portion. Now the Tumbler Ridge Seventh-day Adventist Church meets weekly, welcoming community residents and out of town visitors. Our church membership is small in this busy mining, oil, and gas community—a community needing to know the love of Jesus, needing to see that love portrayed in our lives. As seed-sowers, we pray the Lord of the harvest to send reapers. Maranatha!

C H A P T E R

SEVEN

A Moving Experience

TERRY MARTIN

Behold, I will send you Elijah the prophet before the coming
of the great and dreadful day of the LORD:
And he shall turn the heart of the fathers to the children,
and the heart of the children to their fathers,
lest I come and smite the earth with a curse.
Malachi 4:5, 6

We first met Terry and Judy at one of our seminars in western Washington, just before they moved to their country home. We see them as one of those families that the Spirit of Prophecy refers to as: "A well-ordered, a well-disciplined family in the sight of God is more precious than fine gold, even than the golden wedge of Ophir" (Adventist Home, 32). The three children are well adjusted, musically gifted, and outgoing. They are a great example of the positive influence that country living can have on young people. Here the father, Terry, begins their story.

Terry: After several years of attending family camps, reading books, and talking with friends about the virtues of country living, we decided to attend an "Out of the Cities" rally in Portland, Oregon in 2006. While we had already done some "looking" for country property, after attending the rally and hearing of predicted future calamities, then actually seeing some of those predicted events occur, we decide it was time to move out.

We did a lot of searching for an acceptable country parcel, then identified and purchased one in the spring of 2006. Raw land, no road, no well, no power—but with tremendous potential we all agreed! After completing some "fix up" projects on the house in which we were living, we put it up for sale in February of 2007. The real estate market in the greater Seattle area had already started to "soften", but we set our price and put the matter in the Lord's hands. In July we had a buyer.

Packing It In—Tight

We packed up and moved out to our raw piece of land in our twenty-eight-foot travel trailer, with three kids, two dogs, a horse, some chickens, and plenty of dreams. The first projects included building the road, the well, and putting in power. That done, we had a "pole barn" constructed to serve as living quarters until our home could be built. Within a year, we were in our new home—almost completed—and embarking on the challenges and benefits of country living.

We have learned, largely through trial and error, that the more we trust God, the better off we'll eventually be. Through our own studies and gaining information from outside sources, we became convinced that in the event of a serious calamity, living in the city was very unsafe. In our case, living on the Olympic Peninsula in Western Washington, there were only two ways for several hundred thousand people to exit—one was by ferry boat, and the other over a four lane bridge. It was obvious that both of these routes would quickly become a clogged artery within moments after a disaster. We decided that the only viable safety option was in not living there. If there was a major disaster, there simply wouldn't be enough food, gas, water, or housing to meet our most basic needs. We would be part of a helpless mass of refugees seeking whatever we could find—or get.

Logic told us that it was far better to be a helper, than to be helpless. There were other signs—far short of impending disasters—that "encouraged" us to seek a country lifestyle. Graffiti was plastered everywhere. There were unlimited immoral influences on billboards. Always there was noise—sirens, cars, or someone else's music to distract us. So many influences were fogging our brains that it became more obvious to my wife, Judy, and me, that living in a city, big, middle sized, or small—even if there were multiple exit roads available—wasn't the answer for our children's spiritual safety. Children are at risk in any city. Every night my kids would pray for safety. It didn't seem to me that we were under any immediate threat, but it was enough of a concern to our children to warrant their daily prayer.

Judy and I craved quiet, peaceful, more natural surroundings where we could think, and focus on raising our three children in a safe and healthy environment. We knew that being able to grow at least some of our own food—enough to see us past an emergency store closure—would bring peace of mind.

Misfortunes come—the Bible is clear about that, not only in the Book of Revelation, but in the Gospel of Matthew as well. However, we also know that having quiet time to grow together, in work and play, will make us stronger and more committed to God than would ever be possible in the fast pace of the city.

For years I've heard and read about folks that "packed up and moved" to the wilderness of Montana, or Alaska, or wherever, and I always thought, "Hey, that would be great, but I'm a government accountant, I've got a wife and three kids to support, there's college times three to plan for, and I'm not a twenty-two-year-old single guy, who can grab that adventure."

Impossibilities or Opportunities?

I was pleasantly surprised to discover that God often provides opportunities where we see only impossibilities. When I asked about the possibility of working from home, my employer allowed me the opportunity! I live eighty-five miles from my job site. We are home schooling our two high-school-aged daughters, and my son is doing creative distance learning in his pursuit of a college degree. Is it "perfect"? No, there is only one Heaven and it isn't found on a world map.

The "romance" of rustic living starts to wear off when those around you stop taking thorough showers—a five-gallon water heater in a travel trailer doesn't allow for too many "beauty baths." I find no greater enjoyment than working to build a home for my family, but it is dirty work! To any father I would have to say that among the top five "benefits" of moving to the country and helping to build our own home has been the skills that have been imparted to my son. His "senior class project"—and as a home schooled student he could do this—was to help our contractor build the house; from digging the foundation to nailing the trim on the doors, the concrete work, framing, plumbing,

Left to right: Cami, Judy, Terry, Tanner, Cayce

electrical, and drywall. He has learned skills that will be indispensable to him—the greatest of which is learning how to be a productive, reliable worker. He is now hiring out to other contractors and earning money to help with his college expenses. He can look at our house and know that he had a direct hand in building our home. Plus, he can help others build theirs as well.

It has been such a blessing—opportunity—to our children to be removed from the distracting, damaging influences of the modern, temporal world. We've opted to live without television. The nearest mall is eighty-five miles away. Nobody drives by our house—we're a mile back at the end of the road. And yet our children have an abundance of pure, positive, trustworthy friends from church. They enjoy all sorts of group activities—hiking, skiing, sledding, boating, "game nights"—and they don't mind being under the watchful eye of their parents. I desire only one thing in life—the eternal salvation of my family. Country living, with its blessings (and challenges) allows us to be as close to Heaven as is "earthly" possible.

The key to enjoying this whole experience is in developing a walk with God. Disasters and calamities are going to happen—we are seeing them increase almost daily all around the world. The Bible tells us that in the end things will be worse than we have ever seen before. It also tells us that many will be totally unprepared. Some will be…*marrying and giving in marriage, as in the days of Noah.* We might have the best country house, the best gravity fed water system, even the best garden, but if we don't have a straight walk with God, we will fail of completing the task He has given us.

We are far from perfect, but, as a family, we do start and end our day with God—prayer, reading the Bible, simply listening to His "still, small voice". We return our love to Him by doing as He instructs us. And He provides. I used to have such a hard time cramming all the things I had to do into a weekend—there just didn't seem to be enough hours in the day. Yet, by giving up all "my stuff" and spending my Saturday Sabbath with God, I can accomplish more than I ever would have been able to do on Saturday and Sunday combined!

All the Difference

Moving out to the country was a bold step. Country living is not necessarily easy. Once in awhile, when the going gets tough, I've been tempted to wonder if we did the right thing by moving to such a remote location. When it snows twelve inches, guess who has to plow the road? When a loved one is sick and he is eight hours away, guess who jumps in the car? Life is not "perfect" in the country, but I know that God placed me here for a reason. In His time, more complete reasons are revealed. Out here we have learned to hear His voice—it is just a whole lot easier to hear it in the rustle of the leaves and song of the birds than in the blast of a horn or the wail of a siren.

"Can I do it?" you ask.

I'm tempted to tell you, "If I can, anyone can." After all, I'm an accountant—and we accountants are a pretty conservative lot! If I were to offer advice, based on my experience, I would say:

1) "Stay out of debt" and/or "Have a realistic plan to be debt-free in the shortest time possible". If you are debt free, you will not be required to generate as much income especially if you grow your own food and stay healthy.

2) Find a way to make a living—don't count on retirement. I have a "201K" plan—it started out as a 401K, but it's lost half its value in the past few months. But, don't "write off" being able to relocate simply because your job doesn't seem mobile. Talk with your employer—working out of the home may be a possibility (your boss may just need a little time to think about it). You may need to take time for retraining—start now.

3) Put the matter in God's hands; learn to trust Him, and to know His voice. He is our sure Leader in all our times of trouble. By seeing His provision, now, our faith is strengthened for tougher times ahead.

Cami Says: My family didn't just suddenly decide it was time to move; the process was slow and spread over a couple years of casually looking for property. After the stirring "Out of the Cities" rally in November of 2006, we got serious about leaving the area where we lived, on the west side of Washington. My dad's job required him to live within the state of Washington, so that eliminated the need to look in another state, making our quest a bit easier. Nevertheless, Washington is a large state with decidedly different types of land. We prayed about where we should go and researched the type of land that would best support the growing of gardens and fruit trees.

When Mom delivered my brother, Tanner, and me to the *Young Disciple Youth Bible Camp* near Inchelium, WA, in 2005, she was impressed with the area. She *really* liked the area. That next weekend when she came back to pick us up, she brought along my dad and younger sister, Cayce. Via the Internet, my parents began seriously studying the area north of Spokane, along Lake Roosevelt. We were all excited about getting involved in the property hunt. We prayed for God's leading and He led us to a knowledgeable real estate agent who set us on the right track; he warned us that there were good properties in bad neighborhoods as well.

We planned a trip over to eastern WA and found the "perfect" piece of land: 40 acres of mostly flat land, with woods, meadows, water, power—everything. We called the number on the "for sale" sign—we were exuberant—we found "it"! Our joy was short lived, however because the sale of the property was already pending, soon to close. We were disappointed, but reminded each other that if God didn't want us to have this land, then He had something *better* for us! I'm glad God doesn't just settle for something that's good, or even better, He wants *the best* for us. We took comfort from that promise.

Next to this same property, just a little way down an old road, we found what God truly had in store for us—our "real" property! This land couldn't possibly be pending, because it wasn't even for sale! After several phone calls, this beautiful spread—forty-three acres on the side of a large hill covered in meadows and trees—was all ours! We waited a long time for the right property, but we feel so rewarded for having waited on the Lord's timing.

Even when we had our new property in the country, we still had to learn about waiting. It was not until a year after we found our country property that we were able to put the house we were living in on the market. We prayed for people to come look at our house, to come to our open houses, yet very few people came. We knew the market was on the downside and we knew of no properties that had sold all year in our town. Why wasn't He bringing people? I'll have to admit that there were times that I really wondered if God wanted us to move. I thought that if we were supposed to move, then He could sell our house fast—and the sooner the better. We wanted to be in the country. Once again, God had to teach us the often forgotten lesson of patience.

Toward the end of summer, after well over a month of no interest in our house, a couple came by to see the house and made a full price offer!

"Can you be out in three weeks?" they asked, doubtfully. Could we!

We packed up our things in a hurry and were out in less than the three weeks; small wonder we still can't find some of our things after that hurried packing! We moved our belongings over eight hours east to our new property. When we arrived, the realization hit full force—we had property all right, but no water, electricity, or even shade. It was hot and dusty, and we had no place to put our animals. Fall was almost here, and winter was just around the corner.

Thankfully, we had the travel trailer in which we all lived from August to November of 2007. Five adults, 2 dogs, and a homeless cat (that showed up after we moved) shared the limited space. Thankfully, also, the horse and chickens lived outside! We had *a lot* of trials those first few months: cooking in a camper kitchen, hauling water for everything for a month before the pump was connected to the well, relying on a generator for power, no hint of similarity in schedule from day to day, living on top of each other...and the list goes on. Thanks to the distraction of constructing a pole barn and house, we actually learned to appreciate the closeness.

Before the really cold weather hit, we moved into the four-hundred square foot apartment in our pole building. What a palace! Nothing like living in a tiny place to help one appreciate elbow room! It was finally time to bring over the rest of our pets who were "stored" at Oma's house. When five cats and two dogs moved in to our new apartment, it lost a bit of its charming spaciousness.

About the time we moved into the pole barn, it hit me that I had just moved from the home that I'd lived in for nine years. My childhood bond, that strong chord of love for my old home, was to be permanently broken. The sad reality of never living in *my home* again draped a dark cloak of homesickness over me. I didn't want to let go of what was familiar and I didn't want to let go of my sadness because, in some strange way, that very sadness comforted my bewildered self.

After struggling against depression for a few weeks, I began to sense the need of accepting this new change. Time and time again, I prayed for God to remove my sorrow and replace it with positive thoughts about my new surroundings. I can't say the exact day the miracle took place, but before I knew it, I was "up and running" like my old self. I still missed my old home, but it didn't consume me.

My new church family was one of the biggest positives in the circle of good influences and helped me center my thoughts outside of my own little world. I began thinking about how to help others. This new sense of community completely erased my shroud of homesickness.

The long process of house building has passed and now we dwell together peacefully in our lovely new house… almost *home*. Now, when I go away for trips, I look forward to my return. There really is, like the song says, "…no place like home." I love my new setting with a fierce passion and wouldn't move back to Washington's West Side for a million dollars!

My family has adjusted. We sowed seeds in 2007, trusted God to make them grow, and now we're reaping the harvest of our labors. God has blessed us by providing for our needs, testing and strengthening our characters, giving us health, and a happy family that grows stronger in the Lord every day. He even gave us mission work right at our doorstep! We love our church and are so blessed by godly fellowship—wonderful, sincere youth, and devotedly honest adults. God has given my family so much. I thank Him for watching out for us so carefully.

I have learned that I must even rejoice in the trails (and there are still trials since our family is far from perfect) but, if we rely on Him, we will not fail to overcome. We stepped out in faith and God led us to be able to move to the country. If He did it for us, He can do it for you too!

EIGHT

Sanctuary Ranch Story

LINDA FRANKLIN

www.youcansurvive.org

And I will make with them a covenant of peace,
and will cause the evil beasts to cease out of the land:
and they shall dwell safely in the wilderness, and sleep in the woods.
Ezekiel 34:25

Neither of us would have been completely happy with our college degree and "business as usual" lifestyle while we both longed for a country home. How could we possibly ignore the call to make our home in the wilderness when He threw the doors of invitation open so wide? It was a big step from our city-bred life in Oregon, or even our little country school in Massachusetts, to the wide-open wilderness of northern British Columbia, but we have never regretted our move.

Jere: I first discovered my love for the wilderness back in ninth grade when one of my teachers, Don Van Tassel, took some of the Portland Union Academy class "ruffians" on a camping trip to Lost Lake. It was because of his attempt to reach out to some rebellious teens that my life changed. Though there were some skirmishes that weekend, Mr. Van Tassel, a man among men, separated some of us by literally lifting both fighters off the ground with one arm around each offender. (Don still holds the world's record for holding an eighteen pound Bible at arm's length for two and one-half minutes, the one that Ellen White held, in vision, for one-half hour.) I don't know about how my classmates feel, but I look back at that weekend as the beacon that pointed the way toward my spiritual awakening. I'm sure there were other things that my gym teacher could have done that weekend, but I'm forever grateful that he took the time to show me a better way to live—close to the heart of nature.

After that experience, I often hiked and camped in the woods around Portland. Even the baseball field took second place to my love of nature and her God. It was after I took a guided horseback trip into the Canadian wilderness southeast of Quesnel, British Columbia, that I began to seriously consider living in Canada. The following story, written by my wife, Linda, is an abbreviated rendition of how that dream came true.

Linda: After we were married in 1974, we found ourselves in Massachusetts, leading out in a Wildwood satellite project. While we were there, Jere's mother forwarded us her copies of *The Quiet Hour Echoes*, a church newsletter. In one, she had circled a small two-line ad on the back page: "Farm For Sale In Canada" and a phone number in Escondido, California. When Jere called the number, he learned a few facts about 467 acres on the Sukunka River with portions of good agricultural land, good timber, and an abundance of good spring water and more than a mile of river frontage. Roy and Joybelle were only asking what the property was worth, but it was beyond our reach.

"Well, why don't you see what you can do to raise some money, Jere," Roy suggested. "I'll call you back at this time next week."

Jere envisioned doing for other young people what Don Van Tassel had done for him. In order to accomplish that, the property needed to be in the wilderness. This acreage qualified in every category; remote, agriculturally sound (though challenging weather conditions for growing), and scenic. I suggested that Jere call one of our physician friends to see if he might be interested in investing some money in land. At the very moment Jere called, this doctor and his wife were discussing how to invest a mutual fund that had just matured.

"Go ahead and take what we have here, Jere," said the doctor. "We'll be partners."

Exactly a week later, Roy called back just as we were preparing for bed. Jere reluctantly reported to Roy our limited success at raising the cash. Even with the formation of our new partnership, we were still twenty thousand dollars short of the asking price.

"I can't even really make this an offer, Roy" Jere said.

"You're right, Jere," Roy said brusquely, "that's just not enough money."

Then a female voice interrupted their conversation. It was Roy's wife, Joybelle, on their kitchen extension.

"Now, Roy, let's not be too hasty!" Joybelle explained their financial situation while Jere listened in: they needed a certain amount to pay off their mortgage, they wanted to give a large donation to *The Quiet Hour* (their favorite charity), and then lay aside a certain amount for retirement after taking their long-dreamed-of vacation.

"We'll think about it," Roy said, and abruptly hung up. Jere sighed, shrugged and sat dejectedly down on the bed. I was disappointed, too. Though we were happy in our leadership role at the conservative school in Massachusetts, I knew Jere's heart longed for the wilderness. And there was the fact that he had no replacement to lead out in the project if he was to leave. Perhaps the Lord was saying we should stay where we were?

We crawled into bed with heavy hearts, knowing that our Canadian dream was back to square one. About twenty minutes later, the phone rang, again. It was Roy.

"We've decided to accept your offer, Jere."

Jere stood there with the phone to his ear, looking at me with slackened jaw and upraised eyebrows, unable to say a word. How should he answer Roy? A thousand details would have to fall into place for our path to be cleared, it seemed, but this acceptance of our offer was a big first step down the trail toward the wilderness cabin that Jere had dreamed of for so long. We'd had some practice reading providences. We knew we were on the right path.

"Uh, thanks Roy," Jere finally stuttered. "Thanks a lot! I'll call you back with more information as soon as I can."

Jere plunked down beside me on the bed, smiled a dazed sort of grin, and said, "Linda, they decided to accept our offer..." He repeated that phrase, accentuating a different word each time; "They decided to *accept* our offer! They decided to accept our *offer*! They *decided*..."

Though we had worked in country locations, we felt as though we were walking through a special gateway—property ownership—to our destiny.

Closing the deal on a California-owned Canadian farm from our location in Massachusetts with a lawyer in Tennessee and joint-owners in North Carolina was a logistical challenge! But, far sooner than we ever imagined, we were part-owners, sight unseen (though we had looked at a couple of Roy's pictures), of 467 acres in Northern British Columbia!

Now what? Who would take Jere's place as leader in this little Massachusetts school where so few understood or would be willing to live by the plans outlined by our conservative "mother" institution in Tennessee? Just a couple of days after our "acceptance" with Roy, Jere received a very direct answer for a replacement.

"I really like it down here in Tennessee, Jere," said his friend at the institution that had spawned our satellite school less than a year before, "But our hearts are in New England. My wife and I both feel like transplants down here! I'm having some health challenges and we are strongly impressed that we belong back in New England. Would you have housing available there for us at your school?"

Interestingly, Will was the very man whose name had popped into Jere's head when he first thought about replacement leadership. He had similar work experience and understood the role of leadership in that type of school environment. A few weeks later, Jere and I were free: free of debt, free of responsibilities at the school, had passed our physicals, and had received our landed immigrant status from the Canadian Consulate in Boston. We were on our way!

We left Massachusetts on the morning of our first anniversary. Our long trip from Eastern United States to Western Canada could never be classed as uneventful. Suffice it to say that repairs to Old Betsy (Jere's 4x4 pickup truck) and our home-made trailer depleted our already challenged pocketbook. We limped across the border on May 22, 1975 with less than $100 in Jere's flattened wallet! But we had land, wood, water, a few packages of garden seeds, some dry goods to eat, and a big bundle of dreams. We would survive!

Alone in the Wilderness

It was at twilight on the misty evening of May 23, 1975, that we arrived at Sanctuary Ranch. Tiny, bright green leaves were just emerging on the white-barked aspens that lined the path that was to be called our driveway. We decided to camp right there. Actually it wasn't a choice—Old Betsy was stuck, axle deep, in Peace Country mud! It was nearly dark, so we crawled into our sleeping bags under Betsy's canopy, had a bedtime prayer, and pondered the reality of our situation.

We were alone in the wilderness. We were in wild country; we had already seen moose, coyotes, and deer. We knew there were bears and wolves in this area. We had very little money, and neither of us had a job. We had no electricity for cooking, heating, or lights, even if we'd had a stove, a heater, or a lamp. We had neither sink nor toilet. Our comfort was the knowledge that the Lord had lead us, and that was enough.

Little did we know that first rainy night, camped in the bed of our old Ford pickup, that Sanctuary Ranch would be used for many happy years of surrounding teen-agers with an atmosphere of old-fashioned hominess; wood stoves, water in a bucket, and the peaceful healing of nature's God that flows through the soul from the banks of a woodland river.

As I listened to the soft patter of the spring rain on Old Betsy's canopy that first night, the assurance came to me that I was home. The wilderness held no dread. (I learned, much later, that my paternal grandfather had wanted to move to the Peace Country, but something, or someone, had prevented the realization of his dream.) Though we were both college grads, Jere and I would now be learning lessons in a higher school; The University of Common Sense. And, though we loved nature, in this new school we were to learn a much deeper respect for the power and grandeur of the North and its Creator.

We decided to till and plant the garden first, then work on housing. Our nearest neighbor, Tom, who lived more that a mile away, helped us plow and fence our garden spot, and we planted our first garden. Just about the time we finished planting, Jere went to town for supplies. I was still in the garden when I heard hoofbeats. It was Joyce, owner of the Sukunka Valley Ranch, who lived about three kilometers north of us. She smiled down at me from astride her beautiful bay gelding.

"My strawberry plants need thinning," she said. "You are welcome to have them if you want to pick them up!" Besides an abundance of Joyce's strawberries, our garden produced bountifully that first year. We had bigger onions than I have ever seen in the store!

I named our acreage "Sanctuary Ranch." It was the haven I had longed for since early childhood: plenty of room for housing unwanted animals, surrounded by wild beauty, even our neighbor's herd of colorful and friendly horses. Every week a new foal arrived. Every week, a new bird landed in the spring-green aspens surrounding our cabin. It seemed we couldn't get enough exploration time packed into each new day. It seemed that I noticed color much more as the bluebell-and-wild-rose-pink spring days turned into the long, long summer days of Indian-paintbrush-or-ange-and-fireweed-magenta. I became less aware of time, until I started getting very tired one evening while we were hoeing potatoes.

"What time is it," I asked Jere. "11 o'clock!" he exclaimed. I was used to working "daylight till dark," but summer evenings up north were plenty light for working outside until after 11 pm.

Cheechakos, that's what the local Cree nation calls newcomers during their initiation year. For that first year, and for the next seven years, we lived in a tiny twelve foot square cabin that we reclaimed from miscellaneous wildlife. Our nearest neighbors lived about two miles away, but the roads were often impassable. Tom and Carol proved to be good friends, helping us with practical skills, and even survival during the extreme winter temperatures when our thermometer sometimes hovered at minus fifty degrees Fahrenheit!

Wilderness School

During the spring of our second year, a pastor hiked in to see us (because he was stuck somewhere along our picturesque, but sometimes impassible driveway). He had a suggestion.

"Jere, this place would make a wonderful school," he said, embracing the beauty of the river, the forest, and our garden, with a broad sweep of his long arm. "Have you ever thought of how many kids would just love to live in a place like this?" It was as if he had read Jere's mind.

A week later a single mother brought us our first student, a girl with her few precious belongings barely filling her small suitcase. We had not advertised, in fact we hadn't even had a chance to examine the seed that the pastor had dropped into our hands before children began begging to stay with us. From near and far we received letters (we had no electricity for any other form of communication) from children wanting to come. All we had to offer for housing was a woodshed, a tiny barn, and a boat rack that Jere sided in with some reject waning edge. We named the boat rack Duck Down, because of the extremely low door and it's "coziness."

A proper school, however, must be run by a board. That's how it's always been done, so that's how Jere decided to do it. The board paid us our purchase price, and we forwarded the money we owed to our friends in North Carolina, and signed our property over to a corporation composed of trusted friends and acquaintances. Soon we had students and staff members joining us. We had wonderful (though sometimes economically challenging) times together during those pioneering years. We built log cabins, skidded logs with Caleb and Joshua, our very young and barely green-broke team of Belgians, cut lumber on a donated sawmill to build larger homes and, eventually, built a schoolhouse.

Who needed electricity? Making sure the wood box was full, the water barrels filled, and the meals cooked, created the sense of belonging among the students who lived in family homes. We tried to keep their hearts and bodies warm. Oh sure, there were the usual disciplines, but we had good kids. The harshest disciplines we imparted were what the students termed a "Grizzly Lap" in which the assigned student had to complete a two mile circuit of the grounds after dark, passing pre-determined checkpoints along the way. It is amazing how big a snowshoe rabbit can sound in the deep darkness of a northern winter night! More often than not, a friend or room mate shared the punishment, and often they both returned with a diminished fear of the dark.

Some months were tougher than others, but we always had good gardens and enough to eat. Other than potatoes, we sometimes questioned the trimmings for the next meal, but without fail, we always had more than enough, no matter how many showed up at dinnertime.

The tougher the times, the more dedicated these young people became. We shared with our students some very real needs, and when our prayers were answered (in ways no one could have expected, miraculously, and to the penny more than once!) their faith grew. (Even today, we receive e-mails, letters and phone calls from past students, telling us, "Sanctuary Ranch changed my life. Thanks for being there for me."

The Rest of the Story

How I wish that our Sanctuary Ranch story would have stopped right there, but there were deeper lessons yet to learn. Graduate school? Dark days followed our happy "seven years of plenty". On the eighth year at our wilderness school, we detected a spirit of unrest in a couple of staff families. Jere tried his best to correct the problem, but it remained evasive and underground, an undermining attitude that ducked out of sight whenever he tried to address it. A dark spirit of suspicion permeated our sacred acreage. At last, after the second year of unrest, I requested to address the board.

"Brethren, neither Jere nor I can endure this undermining spirit any longer," I said with a poor attempt at controlling my tears. "You must solve the problem for this cannot go on. Our staff families and students are suffering." I left without suggesting a solution, fearing that my perspective could appear accusatory.

The next day, the board met much earlier than scheduled, and without notifying Jere of a time change. They quickly voted. We were asked to leave. Thus began the darkest period of our lives. We had no "alternative" dwellings to call home. We had put all of our money into the school, including the money that we received for selling the school to the Board of Directors. When we packed up our earthly goods into an old school bus and left the ranch, we felt like Abraham must have felt, that we were going out "not knowing whither we went."

Thus began our search, not just for someplace to call home, but for the place we hoped God would show us to work for Him. We never went hungry, but we were tempted to be discouraged when obliged to live in places that seemed like Sodom for wickedness. Just when I was sure life could get no darker, Jere found a remote cabin in the mountains. After packing and unpacking so many times, I hoped this was our last stop, but four short days after we arrived, even before we were unpacked, our tragedy occurred. We were obliged to take the hands of Sorrow and Suffering, and walk through the Valley of Death itself.

Our son, Jed, then eight years of age, was caught in a gasoline explosion and burned over fifty percent of his body, mostly third degree. For several weeks, Jed's life hung in the balance. This was the most devastating spiritual and emotional turmoil of my life. Three weeks later, when the ventilator was removed, Jed's first words were, "I want to go back to Canada."

Jed had won his struggle against death. For his sake, I tried to find the willingness in my heart to make his "moving back home" wish come true, but I could not rekindle any desire to return to the one place on earth that my son wanted to live, Sanctuary Ranch. It was the one place on earth that we could not go! We had been banished, and I was even afraid to pray about any resolution for fear of God's answer. After all, He had not exactly worked things out in accordance with *my* plans in the past few years! Just as I was stewing about what to think and how to feel about Jed's request, the phone rang. It was a member of the Sanctuary Ranch Board of Directors asking to speak to Jere.

"Hello my brother," I heard the man say as Jere took the phone. "How's Jed doing?"

"He's going to make it, Bill." After a short update on recent developments in our lives, the man, still a member of the Sanctuary Ranch Board of Directors delivered some surprising news.

"Would you consider going back to Sanctuary Ranch? Things didn't work out for the families who stayed behind. There was no vision. Everyone has left, except a family of caretakers. The board has voted for you to return, and to try to and restart the school." He went on to explain that those who had asked for our resignation had apologized for misrepresenting us to the board.

After a stunned silence, Jere told the man about Jed expressing a desire to return to Canada.

"We'll think about it and get back to you," Jere assured the man as hung up the phone with a light in his eyes that I had not seen since the day his dreams had died four years earlier, in the upper room of the school-house at Sanctuary Ranch.

My men did what they could to convince me that it was safe to return. Within a few days I was able to lay my resistance at the foot of the cross. As I prayed, my heart received assurance that the Lord was working things out for us come home.

Though I could speak with the tongue of angels, I could never truly reveal the depth of emotion I have felt about our journey through the dark valley of banishment and broken dreams, nor the far-reaching effects of that fire that nearly killed our son. Destiny does not look like the path we planned, but my heart is at rest, knowing that our home on earth, here at Sanctuary Ranch, is not just our home. It is His heritage to us. He gave it to us— twice! Contacting the same friends who helped us with the original purchase, we were able to buy it again! In less than two years, we were debt-free!

Jed, and his precious wife, Amber, live here at Sanctuary Ranch (read their love story in *Rainbow in the Flames* available from either Amazon, or our book distributor). It is a joy to see our grandchildren growing up, walking the same roads Jed so loved to roam during his growing up years! We thank the Lord daily for His mercies, and His lessons.

It is our desire that Sanctuary Ranch be used to educate His people to use His survival tools until He comes for them in the clouds of glory. And it won't be long, dear friends. It won't be long.

This world is not our home, we're just a passin' through.

Till heaven is our home, what Jesus says is true,

To move where you can grow both character and food
We just can't feel at home in this world anymore.

(Jere and Linda have been holding Family Camps at Sanctuary Ranch
for the past ten years. They also offer seminars in end time events to
churches around the world. For more information go to: www.you-
cansurvive.org)

Oh deep still hills of misty shade
To blue infinity you fade
The tranquil form that you display
Will be a hiding place someday
When weary tears fall to the earth
Fulfill the purpose of your birth
And shield the hunted ones with care
So only God can find them there.

— Cari Strand-Mutch

C H A P T E R

NINE

Northwest Blessings

DENISE SILAS

I will lift up mine eyes unto the hills, from whence cometh my help.
My help cometh from the Lord, which made heaven and earth.
Psalm 121:1

It was during their dilemma about where to move that we received our first e-mail from the Silas family. With much interest we watched their "country home" story unfold. They have made God the center of their family, and we have not heard of a happier family in all of our travels.

It is such a blessing living in the mountains of the Northwest; a life so different from just a few short years ago. Nearly every day I marvel at the miracles that happened so that our family could be out of the city and living in this wonderful country setting!

I was born in Central America. My family immigrated to Brooklyn New York in the 1970's, so most of my life has been spent living in the city. I always felt happy, safe, and privileged to live in New York City. However, things began to change after our first son was born. One afternoon my husband and our baby were on their way home from a stroller ride in the neighborhood and they could not enter our street. The police were making a drug bust. Though we had witnessed things like this before, we now realized it was time to take a serious look at our living conditions.

I immediately began to pray about getting out of New York. About that time a friend retired and moved to Augusta, Georgia. She spoke to us about relocating. She even invited us to stay with her family. We took her up on her offer, and with our four-month-old son we went to Georgia. Within two months we found a nice home to rent, my husband had a job, and we were happily located in a friendly community. Georgia was clean and warm. We grew a small garden and had three more children. We lived from paycheck to paycheck, but we felt blessed to be out of New York.

Promises and Protection

Then the day came that I began to study Bible prophecy. I saw that Daniel wrote about… *a time of trouble that never was since there was a nation.* This made me pay closer attention to the promises in Isaiah about our protection in the mountains and a time when our food and water would be supplied. The more I read, the more I realized that God wanted His children to live in a country setting before we were to flee to the mountains. I came to understand that during the time of Jacob's Trouble, our food and water would be supplied, but that we needed to be in the country in order to provide for our family in the tough times before that time period. It didn't take much effort to understand that it would be to our benefit to have property where we could grow fruit trees and a large enough garden to feed our growing family—it made economic sense for stretching our food budget and would give us healthier choices of food, too!

About this time my husband, Andrew, and I met a family that had sold all that they had and moved to the country with their two small sons. They were not dependent on others for the things they needed to survive, such as food, water, heat, or electricity. Their Exodus experience inspired us.

We began to search the Internet for property but it seemed impossible that we would ever actually realize our dream of country living: 1) we had no home or business to sell, 2) we had no savings, and 3) we desired to stay out of debt. How would we ever finance a property of our own? However, I took courage from the children of Israel's deliverance, reasoning that God was able to deliver them without any resources. Could He not help us, too? My husband and I prayed together about it.

One Friday afternoon, in September of 2007, while bringing in the freshly dried clothes from the line, Andrew and I decided to stop and pray. As we arose from our knees, we were relieved of our anxiety and had a sense of assurance that the Lord was well able to help us. At 7:30 the very next Sunday morning, a friend called and asked, "Are you ready to move to Montana?" I wondered if I was still dreaming as she went on to explain the situation.

The "M" family was house-sitting for the "S" family because Mr. S worked in another state. However, the M family, while there, found a home to buy. So they asked if we could take over the house-sitting! The Lord performed many blessings in order for us to make the move. One example of His provision is the mechanic that He allowed us to meet. The mechanic prepared our 1973 vehicle for the cross country winter trip; the brakes, the tires and engine work (that I don't understand) for such a reasonable price that it really was a gift! Then, angels of the Lord escorted us safely through hard rains, snow, and ice for nearly 3000 miles.

Meanwhile, out in Montana, the M family found out that the home they were buying had a lien against it and they could not move in as planned. This too, was in God's providence. Living with the M family, we learned needful things about life in the mountains. For example, they taught us how to operate the wood heater. We would have been very cold if the Lord had not allowed us some lessons in keeping warm! Though there was no need for two families to house-sit one home, we knew the lien had not taken the Lord by surprise.

While we were living in Montana, another family invited us to spend Sabbath with them. That led to our visiting others nearby. One family knew of a home that was empty. A few days later, we met the owners who lived and worked in another state. To make a long story shorter, we moved from Montana to Washington and became their renters. The home is self-sufficient; the water comes in by gravity from a spring located on a hillside above the house. There is no additional utility bill because we have learned to use solar panels and batteries.

Precious Lessons

Our Christian neighbors are extremely kind and helpful. They have taught us canning, cold climate gardening, sewing on a treadle (non-electric) sewing machine. They taught us to cook and bake using a wood cook stove, and many other useful skills. They also taught the children to ride horses. The blessings have been many; and we have discovered blessings even in the hardships. I think that's called "character building"!

When we first came out to the country, we could not carry a load of wood from the woodshed into the house without being out of breath. Not many weeks after we moved, I saw my 8-year-old daughter smiling as she carried in an armload of wood. She said to me on her way to the empty wood box, "This is the way to heat a home—not the other way—pressing the up arrow!" That was when I realized that she actually enjoyed the extra work it took to warm our house! She felt happy that she could be a part of helping her family be comfortable.

Our oldest son was 10 when we received the call in Georgia that Sunday morning, and he wasn't sure about moving all the way out to Montana. He wasn't exactly afraid of such a drastic change, but all of his extended family and friends would be left far behind. However, before long he could not stop praising God for the wonderful ways He had led us! Our children were 10, 8, 6 and 3 then, and they have never complained about any experience that country living has brought our way. They love it!

Our first two winters in Washington were unusually harsh. We sometimes had to shovel snow from the house to the wood shed, only to have the wind blow the snow back into the trail before nightfall. Sometimes we get cold, but our children do not complain. They know that God is fitting us for His Kingdom and that hardships are a necessary part of that preparation.

Our journey has not been entirely free of challenges, hardships and discomforts, but I realize there will be no perfect environment until we get to heaven. Our family is enjoying our little heaven on Earth, and our character development, too. The lessons are more distinct and personal in the country than in the city. I choose to look at the roses rather than the briers and thorns, firmly believing that the Lord will lead all who are willing to be led by Him.

TEN

Outside the City

DANA WILLIAMS

Call unto me, and I will answer thee,
and show thee great and mighty things, which thou knowest not.
Jeremiah 33:3

Dana and her husband were ready to make a change, but where could they go? How would they be able to discern the Lord's leading? The reassuring signs came just when they needed to know that they were on God's timetable.

My husband, Michael, and I received the "out of the cities" message in February of 2010. We were strongly convicted that it was time to move our family away from the contaminating influences of the city in which we lived. Michael would finish his physical therapy classes at Loma

Linda, California in June. In March we started a small garden in the backyard of our apartment building so that we'd be able to get some experience in growing our own food, which was one of the reasons we wanted to move to the country.

Setting Goals

Our first goal was to be out of southern California by the end of the year. We found out that physical therapists are in high demand in rural areas, because they generally like the conveniences of larger cities and suburbs, so we were very pleased to think it would be easy for Michael to find a job in a less populated area.

We prayed night and day that the Lord's hand would work in our lives and show us where He wanted us to be. About a month after Michael graduated with his degree in physical therapy, I put his resume on the Internet and immediately he began getting a number of calls each day. He was not very happy with me posting his availability because he had not yet taken his board exams. He didn't really want to be talking with potential employers until he had passed his exam. He narrowed the field to three recruiters, two were nationwide, and one who served only the northwestern US.

As we continued to pray, two of the recruiters stopped calling altogether, but one recruiter called one Friday afternoon and left a message stating that she had a position in northwest Washington that paid quite well. Part of our prayer was to pay off our student loan as quickly as possible, so were quite excited about the potential of this job; with this income, we could soon be out of debt. But when my husband called her back on Monday, the position was already filled. However, she told him of a position in north central Washington that didn't pay as much but had a great student loan repayment package.

The company flew our whole family to Washington so that we could check out housing in the area while Michael was there for his interview. Shortly after we arrived in Washington, Michael called his mother back in California to let her know we'd arrived safely. While they were on the phone, an earthquake began shaking his mother's home.

"This is a long one, Michael," said his mother. I saw Michael raise his eyebrows and knew he had learned something significant.

"Maybe we're getting out just in time," Michael said as he hung up the hotel phone. "At least it feels that way to me." We agreed that the time was now and that the Lord had allowed the earthquake as a significant confirmation of our decision to move to the country.

While in Washington, we talked to the local people about the area. It was a different pace than southern California, and we found the people friendly. We felt this was where the Lord was leading us, but even when my husband was offered the job, he was still hesitant to accept the position because he had not yet taken his board exam.

We continued to pray as we returned home, and my husband felt impressed to accept the position. The hospital was willing to hire Michael part-time until he passed his board exams, at which point he would then become a full time employee. A temporary permit would allow him to work at the hospital until that time.

Within a month after flying up for the interview, we would be heading back to Washington—this time with all of our belongings. We were leaving the city, but where would we live? We prayed as we packed. I was in close contact with the only realtor in that small town who dealt with rental properties, and she had repeatedly assured me that there were no rentals available in the country.

Country Rental—A Place to Start

Then, just two weeks before we were to leave, the realtor called and told us that she had found a country rental! It was some distance from town, on ten acres, and seemed ideal for our family. She mailed us a copy of the lease, but warned me that it had been left in quite a mess, so she couldn't promise if it would be ready within two weeks. We felt quite confident that it would be ready for us, and kept packing. The day we received the lease in the mail, I called to let her know it was signed and that we would be sending it back that day with the deposit. She apologetically told me that the owner had decided he'd had enough with renters and was just going to keep the house vacant and put it on the market for sale! It was less than a week before we were to leave for Washington, and no place to call home when we got there!

"Lord," I prayed earnestly, "where will we live?"

Michael called his new boss to let him know what was happening and asked him to watch for a rental for us. The next day he phoned and gave us four phone numbers to call. I spoke with people at three of the numbers, and left a message with the fourth, disappointed that things were not falling into place. Then I received a call back from the man with whom I had left the message. When he returned my call, he told me that he was a realtor. I was disappointed because I knew he didn't deal with rentals.

"I didn't answer your call right away because I was in a meeting with a client who is deciding to take his house off the market and put it up for rent. They haven't had any offers and are leaving the country for a year!" He gave me their contact information. The woman I spoke to happily agreed to hold the house until we could see it!

"Thank you, Lord!"

We finished packing our belongings and headed north. The house was out of town, only an acre, but it had fruit trees and a garden six times the size of the one we left back in Loma Linda! So this is where we are, for now. We know it isn't our final stop, but it's a stepping stone on the pathway to our own country home.

Peace in Providence or Disappointment

You will be interested to know that Michael sat for his board exam about a month and a half after we arrived in Washington. We awaited the results anxiously and both of us were shocked when he didn't pass. He had studied so hard! His work permit became invalid when he did not pass, so he was no longer able to work. We questioned whether we were just moving because we wanted to move or if the Lord had truly been leading us.

While Michael studied, we stretched our budget for another month, praying fervently that the Lord would bless his efforts. We stayed at a hotel in Spokane the night before his exam as it was three hours away from home. I put our sons to bed early and we remained very quiet so Michael could study and pray in preparation for his test the next day. I was impressed to see that Michael didn't seem stressed about this exam.

Michael had a good night's rest, awakened early, dressed, and read a chapter in Proverbs to start his day. When he had finished his private devotions, our sons were still sleeping, so he decided to get breakfast for himself and one of the boys, and bring it back to our room. Then I would go and get breakfast for our other son and myself.

While I was getting my breakfast, I saw two young women walk into the breakfast room who appeared to be Seventh-day Adventists. Looking closer, I saw their mother and recognized who they were! I couldn't believe it! When we got the "out of the cities message", it was through a few different ministries, but one of the videos we watched, *Urban Danger*, played a role in our leaving the city. This mother and her two daughters were one of the families in that same video! I went over and introduced myself and they said they'd like to meet my husband. When I told Michael who I'd seen, he was excited, too.

"Dana," said Michael in a tone of assurance, "This is the Lord reminding me why we are up here. It gives me peace!"

What a blessing that Michael could have this reassurance just before he took his exam! The next day, we paid to get his results online rather than wait for a few days as we had before. He passed!

Seeing the Lord's hand in taking us this far out of the city has really increased our faith. We are so excited to see the home that the Lord has in store for us in the future, but are happy in the meantime knowing that He's brought us out! Our school debt is rapidly disappearing (thanks to answered prayer) and we have had many assurances that He is leading as we surrender our problems to Him.

Running Out

KENYA GUTTORMSON

*To everything there is a season
and a time to every purpose under the heaven.*
Ecclesiastes 3:1

She was twenty-five, single, with no money saved to purchase the little country cottage and garden she'd so often dreamed about. What should she do—sit around and wait? No! Time was running out! The answers she needed were in her old Bible, and in a volume she discovered in a book by Jere Franklin on her Grandmother's book shelf.

"Shouldn't we be moving to the country?" I asked my friends at church. "Shouldn't we live where we can grow a garden and prepare for the

Time of Trouble?"

"We don't have to worry about getting ready," was the response. "There are places already prepared for us. God will take care of us."

Though I had a nagging concern about making a change, the unconcern of my friends and anaesthetizing influence of city living encouraged me to postpone any spiritual preparations. Every beat of my heart said, "Get ready, get ready, get ready". Tight schedules, fast food, drugs, and alcohol were killing my friends—and me, too. I wanted to make healthy choices, but the longing for acceptance with those same friends prevented me from making wise decisions. Yet, with increasing urgency, I was convicted that I must make a change or be among the lost at Jesus' second coming. Stronger and stronger came the warning, "Time is running out". I knew that the warning applied not only to me, but for this old earth, and I really didn't know what to do to be ready. I was almost afraid to acquire that knowledge, for I sensed that I would have to change—everything. After seeking happiness in all the wrong places, I was empty, desperate, and confused. I awakened each morning with an ever decreasing desire to live. What was the purpose of life, anyway?

My godly grandmother had read the Bible to me as I grew up in her home. She told me about some of the events that would take place near the end of time. I recalled something about earthquakes increasing, and fires that would burn out of control. That was already happening. Was there a "plan of escape"?

The Awakening Begins

Shortly after a good friend of mine was killed in a car accident, I fell asleep at the wheel. My car jumped the fence and ended up in a field. The owners of the pasture found me and helped me get to their house. Though I had not suffered serious injury, the gravity of what could have happened overwhelmed me. Was God watching out for me? Did He want me to live? In those few deadly serious moments, a feeling of hope washed over me, and suddenly I knew that I *did* want to live, and that I wanted to change the direction of my life. A close friend was quick to notice the change in my demeanor.

"I think you need to take a spiritual journey, Kenya," he said seriously. I agreed, but knowledge did not give me direction. Life was one big puzzle; I had a few pieces, but I couldn't fit them into any sort of sensible picture.

Time With God

Every day the clock of the Universe awakened me with a louder ticking than the day before. I made a conscious decision to get closer to God. I decided that I would simply spend time with Him.

The time I had spent in partying I began spending with a proven friend—my old Bible. It spoke, personally, to my heart each time I picked it up. I also read, in the first chapter of *The Great Controversy*, about the destruction of Jerusalem. My heart immediately applied this advice to the end times. God's judgments would soon fall, and it was time for Christians to be out of the cities in response to that warning. With that knowledge, my spiritual appetite became voracious.

Within a month, I was convinced of four things that I needed to do: 1) quit my current job, 2) erase *all* the music and video games that I had downloaded onto my computer, 3) end one special and significant relationship, and 4) leave the city. Even if no one else saw any sense in my choices, I knew that I had to follow my convictions. The call was irresistible.

So sweet was my fellowship with my new Friend that I did not sense any sacrifice as I formatted my computer, and quit my job. As for break-

ing off the relationship with my good friend, my heart was broken, but, recalling another quote, I knew it was a salvational issue.

Worldly associations tend to place obstructions in the way of your service to God, and many souls are ruined by unhappy unions, either business or matrimonial, with those who can never elevate or ennoble. Never should God's people venture upon forbidden ground. Marriage between believers and unbelievers is forbidden by God. But too often the unconverted heart follows its own desires, and marriages unsanctioned by God are formed. Because of this many men and women are without hope and without God in the world. Their noble aspirations are dead; by a chain of circumstances they are held in Satan's net. Those who are ruled by passion and impulse will have a bitter harvest to reap in this life, and their course may result in the loss of their souls. (Fundamentals of Christian Education, page 500).

As for the last item on my mental list, getting out of the city, the Lord had a very special plan in mind, but I was still in the dark as to how I would make my escape. Every time I picked up my *Bible* or a *Spirit of Prophecy* book, my heart heard the echoes over and over again: "Time is short; get out, get out, get out."

One evening (whether I was awake or asleep I'm not sure), I dreamed about the Sea of Glass, as mentioned in Revelation 4:6. I looked around me. Everyone had on a white robe. Then, I looked at myself. I, too, was wearing a white robe! For the first time in my life, just for a moment, I felt as if I really belonged, that I was part of that vast, unnumbered throng. Had the scene lasted any more than a few seconds, it seemed as if I would have been consumed by the overwhelming feeling of happiness that accompanied that experience. For a few weeks, I became complacent in that sense of joy, until a devastating newscast flashed across the TV screen.

Time to Run!

"Thousands perish in Haiti earthquake." In those words I sensed a message from God to a doomed planet. People perished that day, not just physically, but for eternity. Shaken, I felt as if I had been floating downstream when I should have been fighting hard against the current of death. Was it too late? Was I lost? Had I floated too far? I needed to get out, or I would be like Lot who waited until the judgments fell close to home. Gone was my joy, even my sense of complacency. I suddenly thought of Noah; he had put everything he had into preparing the ark for the saving of his household before God's judgments fell on a careless world. I wanted to be part of "the plan", the solution, not among those who, at the end of time, would be begging for help too late. There was "an ark to build" to help God's people survive the end times, but who would show me how to implement "the plan"?

The newscast was gruesome. As I sat mesmerized by the rescue efforts in Haiti, the words of a hymn from my childhood pierced my heart: *We know He is near, but know not the day—as spring shows that summer is not far away.*

My heart ached for the Haitian people. It ached for all the lost souls of the earth. It ached for my own issues of rejection that had caused me fall into a mistaken identity. It ached because there was so much I didn't know, and time was running out. It wasn't that I didn't know the "end-time" prophecies, it was because I saw them being fulfilled, and how corrupt the world had become, that made me sense how close I really was to the end of time.

I began to shake. My hands became so weak that I dropped what I was doing. I looked around my room. It was full of stuff. Stuff that I had bought thinking it would make me more acceptable. In that moment my eyes were opened to see that my room held nothing of lasting value. Whatever else happened, I needed to simplify my life. I pulled on my running shoes, and made my escape.

I ran east for several kilometers. I zigzagged through a forest, crossed back country roads, swam through an eerie swamp, and kept running until I ran out of strength. When I finally stopped, I realized that it was a very cold day in January and that I was about to face a night in the woods in wet and torn clothing. I sat down on a bench. An old man who was sitting on the other end of the bench looked trustworthy. I began to talk, not knowing if I was making sense.

"You'll be okay," he said kindly. "Everything will work out." I needed those words.

Organized Exodus

Reluctantly, I returned home. After a day of rest, I packed my car with my books and some bare essentials, and headed east, toward Grandma's house in Manitoba. Two days later, I fell into her arms, mentally, physically, and spiritually exhausted.

Sleeping on Grandma's familiar old couch, I had a dream. This time I was not in heaven, I was in hell. I was tearing at my skin, fighting against the knowledge that I was unable to separate myself from the fleshly desires that doomed me to a lost eternity. I awakened with the strong conviction that no matter how hard I might try, no matter how righteous I might appear, I would never be able to save myself. I needed to know God. I needed to do His will, but I did not have a clear picture. Truth, when I found it, would be about the future, and it would be as important as the numerous fulfilled prophecies in the Bible. It would have to do with how to live in order to help others get through the troublous end times. And, when I found it, I knew I would receive power to live it, but I would need training. Where would I find it?

Finding Answers

Unable to rest after sensing my lost condition, I went over to Grandma's book shelf and picked up a book. It was a book by Jere Franklin entitled ***You Can Survive!*** The cover picture reminded me of the country place where I would like to live. As I read, I dared to dream again about the things that Mr. Franklin was writing about. They were exactly the things I wanted to learn; about Jesus, about gardening, and greenhouses, and natural remedies, and simple living. If only I could live such a life as he described! I would exercise regularly in the fresh country air, and eat right from the garden, learn to know God's voice, and heal in body, mind, and soul.

"My sister gave me that book a couple of years ago, Kenya," Grandma said when I asked her about the book, *You Can Survive!,* the next morning. "You know the Franklins have a family camp out in British Columbia every year at their ranch. Why don't you give them a call?" It took some courage, but finally dialed the number listed. Jere answered the phone.

"Hello?" I said in my smallest voice. "My grandmother, my aunties, and I think we might like to come to your family camp."

"We'd love to have you all," Jere assured me. "Are you working, now?"

"No I'm between jobs."

"Would you enjoy learning about the operation of a greenhouse?"

"I've *always* wanted to learn about running a greenhouse!" I had a difficult time hiding my enthusiasm.

"We are just now beginning our greenhouse season," he said. "Is there a chance that you might be able to come? My wife would love to teach you, and we could use your help!"

Even Grandma's team of Tarpan ponies could not have pulled hard enough to keep me from answering this invitation. Somehow, I knew that this was part of "the plan." I headed back toward British Columbia, arriving long after dark. My bed was ready.

I felt at home with the Franklins. Linda opened the treasures of the greenhouse to me in object lessons such as Christ used while He walked among men. I was physically exhausted, but I could feel my heart growing in grace. Though I wanted to work from daylight to dark, I often had to stop and rest. Though I often would have stayed up late to read, Linda helped me realize the importance of keeping a schedule, especially for eating and sleeping. I had fewer nightmares. Slowly my strength returned. Or maybe it wasn't *my* strength at all! Maybe I was discovering my work and He was strengthening me to do it?

Puzzling Pieces Falling Into Place

I took one step. He revealed the next. Like the man at the pool of Bethesda, I had to decide to step away from my "self"-made bed. The power was not within me to surrender self. It was a gift. For as long as I can remember, I awakened every morning with an ache in my heart. I know, now, that it was the feeling of heartbreak. Now, I awaken each morning with neither heartache nor panic. When I began to understand God's love, that ache started to diminish, and though I still experience times of acute emotional pain, I know that I am never alone. I am a daughter of the King. My worth is in what He thinks of me, not in modeling myself after other human beings.

There was a time when I believed that my worth was in my choice of clothing, what I drank, and being acceptable to my friends. But the real me was in the country, hiking mountains, running on country roads with a dog at my side, stopping for my heart to catch up and listen to that still small Voice that would help me grow into the person I was meant to be, discovering the work I was meant to do.

I know I'm where He wants me to be, and that peace is worth more than any amount of money I could have earned back in the city. I have seen many answers to prayer. Without spending a penny, I have a country home with everything I'd dreamed of having and I am doing exactly what I dreamed of doing. I live "close to the heart of nature," grateful for the daily guidance He has extended to me. With parental love and compassion, and gently repetitive discipline, I am learning to know Him in practical ways. I am sharing my love of country living with others as we present end time events seminars throughout the US and Canada.

He gives "to every man his work." Each has his place in the eternal plan of heaven. Each is to work in co-operation with Christ for the salvation of souls. Not more surely is the place prepared for us in the heavenly mansions than is the special place designated on earth where we are to work for God (*Christ's Object Lessons*, pages 326-327).

I am so thankful for the way that God has led me. If my life had been perfect, would it ever have occurred to me that I needed something better? I can see, now, that He was watching over me from the very beginning, but it was difficult to discern while I was absorbed in my own desires. His plan unfolded, like a protecting comforter. He took me by the hand and helped me advance, in an organized way—not just away from the city, but toward the country and His plan for my life. When the day comes (according to *The Waldenses* chapter in *The Great Controversy*) that I must flee to the mountains, I know that He'll lead me safely, with my hand in His, all the way home, to my *real* home—Heaven.

At the time of this writing, it has been almost four years since my "escape". For so long, life was a puzzle to me, but the pieces are falling into place. God is helping me realize that my true value is reached by allowing Jesus to touch and heal me. I like to think of Him repairing me, like welded metal or a broken bone, so that my weak places might become my strong points, like a reinforced seam.

Speaking of seams—not long ago as I held that favorite old pair of jeans in which I made my now infamous run out of the city, a picture came into my mind.

Hmmm...I could rip the inside leg seams of these old jeans...and from this other pair, I'd have enough material to insert a walking pleat front and back...just a little matter of conversion like Jere wrote about in his recent pamphlet, The Ribbon of Blue...

My favorite jeans are now my favorite skirt! The skirt is an object lesson about how my Father sees me, not as I am, but as I will be, in the fullness of time.

I do sense that time is running out, but instead of panic, my thoughts are lifted upward, my faith is being strengthened by practical living. I am learning natural remedies, harvesting wild plants and making slaves and essential oils (just as I wanted to learn), enjoying my medical missionary home study course (from MEET Ministry), and working in the greenhouse and garden. The sky outside my bedroom window no longer tempts me to dream of some ethereal destiny. Now, when I look at the sky, I think of God: majestic, beautiful, pure, powerful, vast, open, unending, with a heart filled with love immeasurable, and immoveable. He is as anxious to pour His blessings upon me as He is to send sunshine and rain on our gardens. Like a flower of His planting, I want to fill the need for which He placed me here on earth.

I want to be ready for that final season, the Christian's winter. I want to use my preparation time wisely. I want to stand on the Sea of Glass with that vast throng robed in white, just as I dreamed. I want to know that I have done my best to sound the message of God's loving care for me to those who have not heard, to those who might accept the gift of eternal springtime by hearing the story of how he rescued me. Somewhere, in a big city far away, there is a young woman whose heart is empty except for the lost and lonely feelings that once plagued me. One day, maybe I can share God's love with her, in His time.

There truly is a proper season and a time for each lesson to be learned. Sometimes I want so desperately to grow faster, but then I look at our little greenhouse seedlings, "refugees from Eden", resting patiently, growing quietly, getting ready to be used—in His time. What would I change? Like a farmer plowing his field for planting, so the Lord is methodically preparing my heart to receive instruction and discover my work for Him. With daily readings from the Bible and object lessons from my country surroundings, I am growing. If there is one thing I have learned, it is that His timing is perfect. Though time in running out, there will be just enough time for me to get ready.

God never leads His children otherwise than they would choose to be led, if they could see the end from the beginning, and discern the glory of the purpose which they are fulfilling as co-workers with Him (The Desire of Ages, 224).

Home

Len Taylor

For I know the thoughts that I think toward you, says the LORD,
thoughts of peace and not of evil, to give you a future and a hope.
Jeremiah 29:11 (NKJV)

The property Len wanted so badly had been sold right out from under him!
The next property he found looked even better, in fact it was perfect, but it
was not for sale! Should he give up? No, it was, as usual, time for Len and
his wife to pray. As it turned out, Len's plans weren't quite big enough.

When my two children were very young (Gary, age two, and Sylvia Jean
was just nine months), we lived on a busy highway. I grew up in the

mountains and did not like living so near the highway. I wanted a nice quiet place to raise my family. I began searching for a secluded house or lot to buy.

"I Guess I Could"

One day I was riding my motorcycle and noticed a dirt road I had never been on, so I turned onto it. It was just two tracks with grass growing in the middle. Mr. Green, who owned a farm on that road, agreed to sell me a half acre of land and told me that he would have a deed drawn up. When I returned to sign the deed he had changed his mind and didn't want to sell! I really liked the place and had hopes of getting it. It was just what we had been praying for—so private and quiet, with the dirt road and tall pines on the edge of the pond. Wasn't this the place?

I heard that the lot adjoining the farm had nine acres, but was not on the market. I went to see the owner, Mrs. Stark. She said, "I wasn't planning to sell it, but I guess I could."

When Mr. Green heard that I was buying the lot, he offered her double the price we had agreed on. We had not signed Mrs. Stark's contract. Would Mr. Green thwart my plans again?

"No," she told Mr. Green. "I told Mr. Taylor that I would sell to him and I will not go back on my word." The Lord was working it out for me all along, though I didn't know it. The Lord knew the original half-acre I had wanted to buy would be too small for what I would eventually need.

The year after I built my house, my brother and his family needed to move. Since we had plenty of land, they built their house next to ours. When I started a construction business, I needed a storage barn, warehouse, shop and garages. There would not have been enough room on Mr. Green's half acre, but I had more than enough room to expand on our nine acres.

About fourteen years later, my father's health failed and my parents needed to live closer to us. They bought a trailer and we moved it onto the other side of our house, so we could look after them. Mom lived in that trailer for another twenty-five years after my father died. She was ninety-six-years-old when she went to her rest.

Big Enough

Now, fifty years after buying that land, my brother and I have both retired. Together, we reared our children in this lovely, secluded spot with the pine trees and the pond. We were one big happy family. We each had a boy first, then a girl. His son, Larry, is three and one-half years older than my son, Gary. My daughter, Sylvia Jean, was born just three months after his daughter, Theresa. We bought a car together so our wives could drive the four children to and from church school. Lillian took them in the morning and Laura picked them up in the afternoon. We did everything together. Sometimes I wondered how the kids knew which family they belonged to; their fathers were brothers, and their mothers were identical twins.

The storage barn and some of the garages have now been converted into apartments for retirement income. My sister, Pearl, moved here after her husband died, to take care of Mom. She had me build a larger addition onto the trailer to make room for her. It includes more living space as well as a garage and a deck. It's a beautiful bungalow, now. We three Taylor children live here side-by-side in retirement, waiting for the Lord to come.

What a lot of good memories we have shared here! The Lord planned it so much better than I ever could have accomplished on Mr. Green's half acre! I can hardly wait to see what He has planned for us in the New Earth. My brother might even live next door to me! What a God!

"Thank you, Lord!"

Whatever Christ asks us to renounce, He offers in its stead something better. ...Duty becomes a delight and sacrifice a pleasure (Education, p. 296-297).

C H A P T E R

THIRTEEN

Little Cabin
on the Hilltop

Jessica Garrett

That our sons may be as plants grown up in their youth;
that our daughters may be as cornerstones polished
after the similitude of a palace:
that our garners may be full affording all manner of store:
that our sheep may bring forth
thousands and ten thousands in our streets:
that our oxen may be strong to labour;
that there be no breaking in nor going out;
that there be no complaining in our streets.
Happy is that people that is in such a case:
yea, happy is that people whose God is the Lord.
Psalm 144:12-15

You will never meet a family who is more enthusiastic about country living than the Garretts! They have attended our Family Camp in British Columbia and helped with many practical demonstrations of simple living at the Tenfold Advantage Family Camp on the Conference campground in Oklahoma. Here, Jessica, the eldest daughter, expresses gratefulness for her parents' decision to move out before she became attached to city living.

It was Thanksgiving weekend; I was with my parents, Rodney and Desiree, along with my younger siblings, Alexi and Andrew. We were on a horse packing trip in the wilderness enjoying a break from everyday cares and perplexities of our busy lives. I felt as if we had vanished from sight! We were 'way out in the boonies, where nothing but the works of a Master Designer could be seen. It was just our family, our horses, and our dog, Hero. We were enjoying our wilderness route to a favorite hot spring, a nine mile ride from a trail head just outside a tiny Idaho town in the "Frank Church River of No Return Wilderness".

As we rounded a corner of the trail that revealed a captivating view of the enormous snow capped-mountains in the blue distance, our string of pack and riding horses involuntarily paused, as if stilled by the hand of the Creator Himself. The sun glittered across the icy waters of Papoose Creek fifteen hundred feet below the precipice on which we had come to a reverent stop. Brilliant wild flowers danced together in the breeze. After a lengthy pause, our ponies seemed peacefully content with their surroundings, and they resumed their pace. The soft thudding of hoofbeats on a wilderness trail has always been a comfort to me. Perhaps it had to do with Thanksgiving weekend, but suddenly my heart was nearly overwhelmed with gratefulness.

"How did I arrive here?" I asked myself as I relaxed in the saddle. "Why am I so fortunate?" To answer those questions, I will have to look back, fifteen years, to the year 1997.

Difficult Decisions

I was barely four years old. My sister, Alexi, was a darling infant. We had just finished remodeling our house on a couple acres of land just outside of Collegedale, Tennessee. Our parents were facing some difficult decisions.

My mother had spent her childhood on horseback, racing across the pastures of her parents' large cattle ranch in central Texas. My father had spent his earliest years trudging through the swamps of Louisiana searching for snakes, frogs, baby alligators and turtles. Anything that "creeped or crawled" was added to his ever-expanding nature room. My parents were both raised in Seventh-day Adventist families, and, in keeping with their studies about end time events, they were in search of a simpler life. It was as if they had heard a Voice behind them challenging them to raise their family in less inhabited regions. They read through books by Ellen White, such as *Child Guidance* and *Country Living*, and were strongly impressed that the time to make their move to the country was now, before I could become attached to a city lifestyle.

Better than any other inheritance of wealth you can give to your children will be the gift of a healthy body, a sound mind, and a noble character. Those who understand what constitutes life's true success will be wise betimes. They will keep in view life's best things in their choice of a home (*Country Living*, page 15).

My parents were tired of *dwelling where only the works of men can be seen* (*Adventist Home, page* 131). They were ready and willing to *go where they could look upon the works of God. Find rest of spirit in the beauty and quietude and peace of nature. Let the eye rest on the green fields, the groves, and the hills. ... Go where, apart from the distractions and dissipations of city life* (*The Ministry of Healing*, p. 367). And they strongly believed the admonition; *...give children your companionship, where you can teach them to learn of God through His works, and train them for lives of integrity and usefulness* (*The Ministry of Healing*, 367).

"Before they call..."

Mom and Dad put our house up for sale, desiring to list it in the real estate book, but before the ad was even printed, a friend of ours bought the property! We packed furiously and moved to Texas where Daddy

Back row, left to right: Alexi, Andrew, Jessica; front row, left to right: Rodney and Desi Garrett

was promised a commercial plumbing job. Three months later the job fell through leaving us searching for other options.

Pulling out a map, we saw that Idaho had lots of National Forest. Idaho County was a place we had previously heard was very respectful of home-school and country-minded folk, so we planned a week long trip north. We searched property after property, and counseled with realtor after realtor, but no description fit what we wanted. On our way home, we saw a tiny log cabin with a realty sign on the porch. The surroundings were bare, rocky bluffs, beautiful in their own way, but the land just was not in keeping with our picture of "the right place." The cabin became our reason to pull out our list of "must haves." We repeated them to one last realtor from memory, "We are looking for a piece of property that has timber, pasture, water, no buildings, and no close neighbors. Difficult access is not a problem, but we'd like a good growing season, and National Forest borders are a plus."

"I have several pieces that fit your description," he smiled. "I'll show them to you in the morning."

That evening we pitched our tent at a local campground just outside of Riggins, Idaho. Alexi and I quickly spotted some apricot trees and began to climb the branches seeking the plump, heavenly fruit. Bright and early the next morning after mom had cooked a scrumptious breakfast on our campfire, we headed out to meet the friendly realtor. We piled into his truck, crossed the Salmon River, and began winding our way up a creek bed. We saw an abundance of blackberry bushes towering beside the road. Up and up we went. Just when we thought the road was barely good enough, it turned into an old logging road with a twenty-seven percent grade, a drop off on one side and cliff on the other. We bumped our way safely to the top. What we saw made us catch our breath.

This Is Home

The view was stunning! Miles of mountains rose majestically as far as my little eyes could see. There were trees so big it took our whole family, hand in hand, to reach around them! Water was abundant, and the pastures were thick with grass that grew higher than my head. Blackcaps, better known as black raspberries, were profuse; their juicy sweetness soon stained my fingers, face, and clothes with sticky, purple juice as I stuffed handful after handful into my mouth. My sister was quite a mess, too! But oh! How yummy! Our family fell in love—at first sight—with that remote piece of wilderness. Dad quickly made a down payment and hit the road for Texas in great anticipation of the life to come!

Five months later, in November of 1998, we drove our only vehicle, a rebuilt 1975 Scout, loaded with belongings, out to our new home in Idaho. Just after arriving in Idaho, the transmission blew and we were forced to stay in the Hoots Hotel while trying to fix our rig. We quickly realized just how far out we really were when we couldn't find a rental car closer than a two hour drive from the nearest town. The parts we needed wouldn't be arriving for several weeks, and there seemed to be absolutely no mechanics in the area. Here we were, so close to our destination, but stranded. What could we do?

One is sometimes tempted to despair when life looks dark, but that is just the time that God expects us to do our part, and be receptive to the One who is more than willing to plant and nourish that tiny little "mustard seed of faith". We planted that tiny seed in our mountain of problems and waited, helplessly, on the Lord. As we prayed we saw the path unfold in front of us. It was one of those character building opportunities we read about so often, only this was real life, with tangible problems, not someone else's predicaments. Our string of troubles from those early days of our "escape" we now recount as ribbons of blessings.

Country living has taught me, along with common sense, many spiritual lessons that I so much need in order to be mindful of the things of heaven. Without these opportunities I would not have learned to perceive how the Lord works things out for our good! God *did* have a plan. He *always* does! There are so many wonderful quotes to remind us about His willingness to strengthen our faith in the process of building our character:

The faith that strengthened Habakkuk and all the holy and just in those days of deep trial was the same faith that sustains God's people today. In the darkest hours, under circumstances the most forbidding, the Christian believer may keep his soul stayed upon the source of all light and power. Day by day, through faith in God his hope and courage may be renewed. ... In the service of God there is to be no despondency, no wavering, no fear. The Lord will more than fulfill the highest expectations of those who put their trust in him, He will give the wisdom their varied necessities demand.... We must cherish and cultivate the faith of which prophets and apostles have testified—the faith that lays hold on the promises of God and waits for deliverance in his appointed time and way" (Maranatha, page 66).

"Courage, energy and perseverance they must possess though apparent impossibilities obstruct their way, by his grace they are to go forward. Instead of deploring difficulties, they are called upon to surmount them. They are to despair nothing, and to hope for everything. ...For the disheartened there is a sure remedy, —faith, prayer, work. Faith and activity will impart assurance and satis-

faction that will increase day by day. Are you tempted to give way to feelings of anxious foreboding or utter despondency? In the darkest days, when appearances seem more forbidding, fear not. Have faith in God. He knows your need. He has all power. His infinite love and compassion never weary." (*Christian Service*, pages 107, 235)

From Despair to Hope

Just before we lost hope that day (when we were just beginning to learn about how to build our character without despairing), we were introduced to a local mechanic who happened to be a Seventh-day Adventist. In picking a country home we had not even considered who our Idaho church family would be, but we were led right to the very place where we would meet the fine folks who became close friends and taught us exactly the practical skills we would need to live the life we wanted to live. This family reached out to us and took us "into their heart and under their wing". We are ever so grateful for all that we learned from them!

A man at the motel where we were staying offered us his station wagon as a rental car, this was a huge blessing, for now we could travel—if we dared—just a little! Our "loaner car" was an ancient tan colored, rusty vehicle with nearly all the windows busted out, dents and bullet holes aplenty, but, by this time, appearance did not matter much. We gladly accepted the offer of four wheels with a working motor. I found it great fun not needing to open doors in order to get out of the car. Why do that when you can tumble out through a window? The folks at Hoots Hotel were kind to us, but I was literally bouncing off the walls in our room; window sill to bed created a great trampoline effect. Our vegetarian options were extremely limited at their tiny restaurant; the fare consisted largely of tomato soup, Tater Tots, and baked potatoes.

Often, through my growing up years, I heard my father repeat these words, "If nothing's stopping you, you'd better check your map. The Garrett's don't travel the easy path!" This ordeal with our car may have been the first time I heard him use the expression. We pressed on, eating Tater tots and tomato soup for several days, and searching for the light at the end of the tunnel.

Our original plan was to rent a house near our property while we would plant orchards, develop spring boxes (concrete or plastic box that collects water from a spring so that it can be directed into pipes), and build our house. However, there simply were no houses for rent anywhere in the vicinity, not even fixer-uppers. This left us putting our belongings into storage and waiting at Hoots Hotel.

Daddy called a family meeting. Mommy expressed her usual optimism.

"Rodney, let's just move on out to our farm!" She was almost glowing. "We all love being outdoors! Camping is so much fun, and it will be good for us to be in the back country." Daddy looked amused, as usual, at her enthusiasm. What would our family have done if Mom had not been healthy and optimistic? I think those are the traits Daddy admires most about Mom, but, as head of the household, it was his responsibility to keep us safe.

"Desi," he said, "It's the middle of November! There is no house. Snow has already fallen!" There was a dramatic pause before he hesitantly added, "But…if you want to…well, I'm ready for an adventure!"

Mommy was ecstatic! Without hesitating she blurted, "Let's go!"

Housing ideas flew in from all four directions: teepees, wall tents, pine bow forts—what to choose? Everything sounded like a blast to me! I was ready to get out of that motel! As night settled in, Alexi and I piled onto our parent's bed. The four of us played and talked as usual, but this time we came to a momentous decision about our new house. It would be made of straw! Just plain straw bales. Nothing fancy, since time was of essence, there would be no stucco or foundation. This plan would enable us to move to our property immediately.

Straw House Winter

The next day, we borrowed a truck and trailer and bought one ton of straw bales to stack up for our new house. We unloaded and stacked the bales into a square about twenty feet long and fifteen feet wide. By noon, the walls were complete. After returning the truck and trailer we strapped tin onto the top of our handy-dandy (sputtering) station wagon and once again encouraged the rickety rattletrap up our steep, icy driveway. Daddy arranged the tin over the straw bales and weighed it down against the wind with various heavy objects we had on hand, including our tires and wire. While Alexi and I were romping outside in the fresh snow, Mommy created a door by hammering nails through a blanket and into the doorway "header" board. This prevented the chilly breeze from blowing its flurries too far inside our new abode.

Daddy hauled in a tiny quaint fireplace, setting it on plywood to keep the fancy legs from sinking into the wet ground. Alexi and I helped him hold the rusty stove pipe as he screwed it together and stuck it through the bales. We packed loose straw around the opening to keep the friendly drafts from inviting themselves in. We did realize this could very well be a fire hazard, but we thought the smoke would not to cause too much trouble because it would be cool enough by the time it reached the bales. Besides, our fireplace was so small that it required constant stoking just to keep it burning. On the occasion when we were not at home, our fire would be out cold. (We would learn that a little more care might have prevented "the accident," but more on that later.)

Alexi and I broke open a few bales and, fluffing up the straw as a bed, we curled up together with our pit bull terrier, Blue, and felt quite at home in our new winter wonderland. Daddy went to cut some trees for firewood while Mommy worked on arranging her kitchen. It was to our advantage to give her room to work, for Alexi and I would soon be getting hungry!

Mommy has always loved culinary arts, and she needed a place to create her masterpieces. First, she went outside and picked up some cinder blocks. Then she dug into the snow to retrieve several rough-sawn boards of various lengths and thicknesses, wiped off the snow, and brought them inside to dry. Two rounds of firewood served as the base of her counter. Cinder blocks were placed on top of the firewood, and those wet, rough boards made her new counter a workable height. Out came a select few cooking utensils; one big pot, a cast iron skillet, a two-burner propane camp stove, two oil lamps for light and, of all things, a popcorn popper! (If there is one thing the Garrett family loves it's popcorn!) Our refrigerator was very handy; we just set the food outside our front door in the snow bank! Potatoes, onions, carrots and other roots kept well underneath the countertop near the door where they were cool but not freezing. A couple of rubber tubs contained other staple food items.

The sun was setting on John Day Mountain when Daddy returned with his load of wood, and before nightfall our little pot-belly stove was heating our new home. Then Daddy unloaded our generator and pulled some extension cords inside so that Mommy could use her kitchen appliances to fix supper. We even had a light bulb in the middle of our hut, but it only worked when the noisy generator was running; which ruined the quietness of our wilderness dwelling. As that eventful day came to a close, our stomachs were warmed by Mommy's home cookin'. It was a long day, but, oh, how happy we were to be out of the motel, in the place our hearts will forever call "home"!

That night, and for many nights to come, our bedroom bales doubled as our playroom; we had wrestling and tickling matches, and we rode a bucking bronco (better known as "Daddy") whenever we could coax him into giving us a ride on his back.

As each happy day came to an end, Alexi and I received back rubs from Mommy while Daddy read us highly animated Bible stories. We snuggled together on our hay bed and dreamed happy dreams. I would wish every child on earth could know such happiness as I knew during our "straw house winter".

Sudden Storm

One windy night, I was sound asleep on my straw bed when I awakened to hear the wind roaring down the mountainside. I could hear it screaming through the trees just before it hit our house. The tin on the roof flapped and rattled angrily. Just as quickly as it came, it was gone, rumbling away in the distance as it swept through the canyon below our little homestead. A few minutes later, I again heard a faint howl that grew louder and louder until I heard, "Whoosh-bang!"

All of a sudden we were sleeping under the stars! A gust of wind tore our tin roof right out from under the tires, along with the rolls of wire and several other heavy objects with which Daddy had secured it, sending it our tin roof sailing across the field.

I heard another gust building momentum. Daddy jumped over to Alexi and I just as the back wall of stacked bales came toppling down! The other walls followed in close succession.

"I guess we'll have to rebuild our house in the morning!" Mommy said sleepily.

"No, Hon," Daddy replied, pulling on his clothes in the darkness. "We have to get the tin tonight, before it goes visiting the neighbors!"

There was just enough light so that I could see the recovery operation. Like an eaglet in the depths of my warm straw nest, I watched my parent-birds glide across the cloud-like snow fields desperately gathering the remnants of their nest. Fighting the gusts of wind for possession, they'd fly as far and as fast as they could, then grab their prize and sprawl out on it and to keep it from being reclaimed by the wind. Gust by gust, piece by piece, the stray tin was restored to the vicinity of our bales and weighed down. Mommy and Daddy climbed back into their bed under the stars until morning.

After that incident we made a trip to the hardware store in our rickety station wagon and got some re-bar which we bent into large staples. Re-stacking our house, we stapled those ornery bales together, and they never again came apart!

Staying Warm

Since we had arrived in November, with no firewood on hand, we hooked our toboggan to the back of our small tractor and bundled up in a regular mass of clothing. Alexi and I would go "hooky-bobbing" on the toboggan behind the tractor, up the hill, and into the trees. After cutting and loading our fill of wood, we would sit on top of the load as Daddy headed back down the hill to enjoy a nice, warm, slow-burning fire.

Wet, green wood does not burn fast or hot. The heat in our little hut was sufficient but not overly warm. About this time our realtor informed us of a sawmill yard where we could collect dry slabs for free, we liked that idea. Mixing the green and the dry wood together, our little stove glowed with true warmth.

One night, when our fire was roaring (maybe we had a little too much dry wood in the mix), Alexi and I sat spellbound as Daddy related stories about his adventures as a child growing up in the swamps of Louisiana.

"Tell it again!" we would say as he finished each story. "Tell it again!" So he would. In the midst of retelling one story, I was distracted by a faint red glow around the chimney. I was certain the bales had caught fire. When I was two years old, our neighbors' house burned to the ground and I was afraid of house fires after that. Finally, after what seemed like an eternity, I convinced my Grandpa, who was also in the process of moving to our property, to check on the condition of the chimney. Story-telling and popcorn eating came to an abrupt stop.

"Fire! Fire!" The word spread quickly. We began pulling, pushing, and prying on the bales, almost regretting our great stapling job! Close by was a large mud puddle which served as a place to dunk the ignited bales. We lost about one-third of our bales to fire that night. The next day our rebuilt our house was much cozier—due, in part, to a significantly reduced amount of building materials!

Staying Clean

Mommy had a rather large laundry to do the next day as she scrubbed the blackness out of our fire-fighting clothes. Laundry day was always interesting. After scrubbing our clothes in five gallon buckets and rinsing them in the toboggan, we would hang them up to dry across the boards inside the hut that held up our roof. With clothes hanging around, it was nearly impossible to walk, or even see each other, for that matter! It was on these days that we always had the most visitors, or so it seemed. We sat on the floor, under dripping wet jeans, and welcomed our neighbors, realtors, and other people who popped in to check on the "new family" who had moved from Texas to Idaho in the dead of winter, stacked a straw bale house, and were living there with two little girls. Apparently, we were the talk of the town.

Now you are probably wondering what we did for baths. Just down the hill from our little straw hut was a big black horse trough. It was filled and running over with spring water. Ice covered the ground and grass where the water cascaded down the slope. In order to be submerged, a body had to break the glassy glaze that covered the trough. Needless to say, a bath in that trough was invigorating! No hot and cold water— just cold, colder and coldest! After a "winterbath," one felt *seriously* clean; not exactly relaxed, but very much alive! That's where Mommy and Daddy took their baths. They never stayed down there for very long! They'd come flying back up the hill to our straw house, riddled with goose bumps, bath towels a-flying, duck through the blanket-door where Alexi and I were playing, all snug and happy, and attempt to calm their wildly beating hearts. While they toasted themselves at the fireplace, they'd relate their latest icy drama through chattering teeth. Alexi and I had warm, comfortable baths for what seemed like hours on end with me in our plastic, boat-shaped toboggan and two-year-old Alexi in a five gallon bucket. Mommy melted snow on the wood stove and poured it into our bath tubs whenever our water cooled down. I was thankful for warm water, but I remember wanting very badly to be "big enough" to take my bath in the trough, too!

Growing up a Garrett

Another vivid childhood memory comes to mind. I was ten years old, still unsure of interacting with the public, when I learned a valuable lesson in perseverance. Daddy had remodeled the original old homestead log cabin, and then "selectively modernized" it with a few conveniences which included a phone. While I was at my grandparent's house, helping with chores, a wonderful idea formed in my mind about how I could "improve my talents", so to speak. Grandpa said I could use his phone, so I called Mommy right away, unable to contain my enthusiasm.

"Mommy! Mommy!" I yelled excitedly into the receiver, "Alexi and I have $250! We could buy a hundred hens and sell all the eggs to Mr. R. We could make lots of money!"

 "Find a hatchery," said Mom, matching my enthusiasm. "Ask their advice about the different breeds. That will help you decide which chickens would do best in our climate and they can ship the chicks to you."

She knew I would balk at the idea of talking on the phone to anyone other than family, but she sensed that this idea of mine could serve to stretch my boundaries. Mommy and I had a rather heated discussion about how she could do this for me, but she maintained her calm insistence. I thought about this new venture for quite awhile, and finally gave in to the fact that if I really wanted to raise chickens, I'd have to order the chicks myself. Finally, after a significant delay, I picked up the phone and dialed the number for the local hatchery. I stammered and stuttered, fumbling over my words, but eventually settled on a final price for 100 Golden Sex Link pullets. From beginning to end, raising chickens was a lesson in perseverance; a very worthwhile lesson.

My parents never squelched our desire for adventure. Whether in the world of business or the great outdoors, they joined right in on our "wacko escapades", regardless of how crazy and foolish they might have appeared. They'd take our original idea and turn it into a learning experience, offering suggestions, teaching us about maintaining our Christian experience in dealing with others. They seemed to thoroughly enjoy the world of young hearts.

As we grew, so did our knowledge of animals, animal husbandry, and an appreciation for the wilderness. Our feet and our horses took us miles into the vast territory beyond our homestead. We identified mushrooms, followed bears to their dens, searched for our ever-escaping sheep, chased wild turkeys until we caught them with our bare hands, and quietly slipped into a world of trust in God as we watched the clouds drift across the sky, and listened to the birds fill the forest with their songs.

I'm so appreciative that our parents taught us how to work and not to give up just because a job looked overwhelming. We were given tasks equal, but challenging, to our age and strength. We were taught to "keep going" no matter what obstacle we might meet. I recall, as a little girl, standing by the sink washing dishes and complaining about oatmeal being stuck to the pot I held in my soapy little hands. Mommy called out, "Just give it some more elbow grease." With her non-judgmental words ringing in my ears, I'd scrub away. The pot, eventually, came clean. I had finished my task. Perseverance and determination pushed me just a little farther, faster, higher so that I had just enough confidence to tackle a new challenge. Insurmountable odds? Probably not; not if it's something God wants me to accomplish in His strength.

From the time we were just toddlers, our parents set boundaries. When we went beyond our abilities, the natural result followed. We would sometimes even injure ourselves. In this way, they "protected" us without constantly sheltering or "nagging" us. We were nearly impossible to keep track of! So long as they believed we could endure the troubles we were in, they didn't help us out, cushion our falls, or pad our pathways. They realized that character is formed by enduring difficulties. With that in mind, they let us in on the "secret struggles" of the family. We were involved in the hardship, the excitement, and the work that brought food to our table. We knew beyond the shadow of a doubt that we were needed. Who else had time to collect the eggs, bake the bread, weed the garden, feed the dogs and rabbits, and feed, water, trim, and exercise the horses? We learned to use our hands, to figure things out, to "do it" ourselves. And we loved it!

My parents loved me and my siblings so much that they were unwilling to do for us what we could do for ourselves, even when it would have been easier for them to do it. Our parents' lives revolved around us kids, wherever they went, we went. Whatever they did, we did. No matter how menial or significant the task, they showed us how to do it. If we asked questions, they always answered. Sometimes we would catch them off guard and stump them. Then they taught us to use dictionaries and encyclopedias, and we learned together.

I can remember going to the dumpsters in search of broken appliances. Out of curiosity we would take them apart. Amazingly, some of the irons, sewing machines and stereo sets became useful after our little fingers were done rebuilding our "treasures". But more often than not they were returned to the dump in a million pieces, our inquisitive minds satisfied with the exploration of new parts.

Time and space do not allow me to relate the hundreds of other stories, unforgettable memories that amuse our family with the retelling. Suffice it to say, I thoroughly enjoyed my childhood. I have no regrets. Yes, I *was* deprived—of boredom! No cell phones, computer games, movies, or plastic toys cluttered our home. They were replaced, more than tenfold, by horses, sheep, dogs, chickens, four-wheelers, tractors, sleds, rafts, trees, fields, sewing machines, spinning wheels, and an endless array of tools that we learned to use. No matter how busy the day, it seemed that there was time to stop and watch the clouds.

Looking back over my first twenty years, I cannot begin to fully express the gratefulness in my heart that my parents were willing to follow God's call, putting aside their aspirations for worldly gain and laying their all on the altar for my siblings and me: their friends, family, funding, and reputation. Our life was not easy, but all good things have come our way. We are stronger children for the efforts required of us by living a simple country life. The more acquaintances I make, the more thankful I am for my parents' enthusiasm about simple living.

It is my wish that every child could experience the upbringing that I had—filled with rough-and-tumble adventure. I would urge every parent to make their move to the country (regardless of cost in terms of self, time, or financial investment) before your children are old enough to become attached to this world. And don't take the city with you into the country when you move, either! Replace your present choice of entertainment with wholesome, outdoor, hands-on practical skills. Parents, play with your children, walk with them, and work right alongside them. They will "rise up and call you blessed," just as I do this day. My parents are not only my best friends; they are my guides to practical living, and my spiritual counselors for the life to come.

Staying Together

By living in the country, daily depending upon each other for our necessities, our love for each other and for country living, has grown by leaps and bounds. We learned so many lessons by trial and error. Together, we have doubled over with laughter at our failures. We have cried together over our losses. We have encouraged each other in times of physical hardships. We have prayed together for strength to endure trials and memorized Scripture passages to help equip us for trials to come. We have skimped and eaten inexpensively, but never have we lacked necessities. During our several financial crises, trying desperately to "make ends meet," Daddy would gather us together to pray for divine intervention. More than once, within minutes, the phone would ring offering him a new business option! I can recall one time when eight options came through in one day! Another time, our whole litter of puppies sold—all in one morning!

Our favorite Bible text is now: *I have been young, and now am old; yet have I not seen the righteous forsaken, nor his seed begging bread* (Psalm 37:25). When I look at the world around me, I feel so rich: rich in family, rich in land, rich with flocks and herds, rich in practical useful skills, and spiritually enriched as well. We three children have had so many advantages that we would not have had if our parents had chosen to live in our more "convenient" home back in Tennessee.

After our "straw bale winter," so many years ago, we traveled together and worked on commercial plumbing jobs for several years. Between jobs we worked on our land and remodeled the log cabin originally built by settlers in the 1890's. We have added orchards, gardens, fences, buildings, houses, roads, and even a little brother, Andrew, who was born in our log cabin in 2001! We are still as excited about living in the country as we were fifteen years ago. It is our desire to help others in their trek into the wilderness find joy in their journey and experience the same vibrant life that we enjoy so much. I wonder if I feel a little bit like Jesus might have felt about his country home.

*Jesus came to this earth to accomplish the greatest work ever accomplished among men. He came as God's ambassador, to show us how to live so as to secure life's best results. What were the conditions chosen by the Infinite Father for His Son? A secluded home in the Galilean hills; a household sustained by honest, self-respecting labor; a life of simplicity; daily conflict with difficulty and hardship; self-sacrifice, economy, and patient, gladsome service; the hour of study at His mother's side, with the open scroll of Scripture; the quiet of dawn or twilight in the green valley; the holy ministries of nature; the study of creation and providence; and the soul's communion with God—these were the conditions and opportunities of the early life of Jesus (*Adventist Home*, page 132).*

CHAPTER

FOURTEEN

A Willing Sacrifice

AMY JENNINGS

Train up a child in the way he should go:
and when he is old, he will not depart from it.
Proverbs 22:6

After being subjected to the message of country living, Buck and Amy won-
dered, "Is it really so important to live in the country?" Laying their plans
before the Lord, they questioned if they might be hoping for too much. Sur-
prisingly, the Lord seemed to reword their inquiry and toss it right back,
"The real question should be what are you willing to sacrifice for the salva-
tion of your children?"

Our home was in the suburbs of Seattle—a modest house in a nice

197

neighborhood. Our church had recently moved into a fine, new facility. My husband had a good job as an accountant for a large company. By most people's standards we had it all. But something was missing— a connection with Christ that would make a difference in our family and provide a better spiritual atmosphere for our children.

We became increasingly aware of the need to redirect our lives from centering on our own wants and needs, to God's goals for our family. We understood this connection with Christ to be vital. The desire for our family to be in the kingdom became uppermost, for if even one person in our family would miss heaven it would be one too many. As we studied, it became more and more clear to us that our children were to be our first work. The Bible commends us to raise them "in the nurture and admonition of the Lord" (Ephesians 6:4). The character development of our children was more important than the "things" that the world tells us we need, or what church friends might suggest or even what we think we can't live without! Though we need to work for the salvation of souls, our first work, as parents, is the salvation of our children. Our children are with us for such a short time, but we can easily be diverted from salvational issues. Impacting their lives for good while they are with us is of primary importance; "For what will it profit a man if he gains the whole world, and loses his own soul?" (Mark 6:36). What if we gained converts and lost our own children?

Asking Questions

We asked ourselves a series of questions: How do we get that vital connection with Jesus—the kind we seemed to have when we were newborn babes in the faith? How do we transmit that faith to our children? Would the reading of Bible stories to our children each evening and taking them to Sabbath School be adequate? We received the distinct impression that living our suburban lifestyle was too often at cross purposes to their receiving the crown of immortal glory.

A serious search of the Bible and the Spirit of Prophecy was our springboard enabling us to ask intelligent questions of couples and families that had children who demonstrated the "good fruit" we so desired to see in our own lives and the lives of our children. The Bible says, "By your fruits ye shall know them," so we became fruit inspectors of sorts. We knew it would be improper to attempt to judge the motives of those whose children we would not want ours to emulate, but we eagerly began asking questions of those parents whose children appeared exemplary. "How do you do it?" we asked them.

The answers were consistent; "Eliminate distractions."

Accepting Answers

We saw the need for some drastic changes in our lives to supply our children with more lasting value system than living for the things of this world. They needed to spend more time in natural surroundings. We realized, with regret, that we had been fooling ourselves in reasoning that we were living a spiritual life in the city. It seemed to us that when we live in the cities (suburbs, too) we are in Babylon, or confusion. We were being affected negatively, whether we realized it or not. As we sought answers we had to admit the truth; our surroundings prevented us from focusing on Jesus. We realized that, in order to put God first in our family, we would have to make a serious change, but how would the children feel about such a change?

Fortunately, our children have always enjoyed nature and the countryside. We lived in country locations when we were first married, but the pull of making a good living and having the comforts of the easy life tugged us back into city living. Living in the city increased our appetite for the country, especially after reading the pamphlet, *Country Living*, by Ellen White and other back-to-the-land publications. But we discovered that making the break was harder because we were used to the ease and comforts to which we had grown accustomed. We found ourselves struggling to see through the thick fog of 'big city life' near Microsoft Mecca. It was during this time of indecision that some church friends approached us with a proposition.

"A group of families from our church are going to attend a Family Camp meeting in Eastern Washington this year," they said. "Would you like to come?"

As new parents of our little Rachel we were eager to obtain any encouragement in parenting that we could find. We immediately said yes. The experience was life changing, more than can be shared here. The issue

of country living was thoroughly discussed. We learned that it is ten times easier to raise children in the country than in the city. All of the counsel that we had read years ago in *Country Living* came flooding back to us, bringing with it another wave of conviction. The Lord used this experience to speak to us loud and clear. We needed a new direction, and we needed to hear His voice. My husband and I realized that it was just too difficult for us to find that essential "quiet place" in our city setting. We must do something, and soon.

Shortly after the Family Camp meeting, we received word that a big rally about country living was being held in Portland, Oregon. We were excited about what the Lord would open to our understanding, and we were not disappointed. We returned from that trip with some answers as to, not just *why* but *how* to leave the city. With renewed determination we decided it was time to make a clean break from the deceptive life we were living.

Dark Providences

In 2003, God gave us a boost toward a drastic change when my husband's company down-sized. Buck was laid off! We had already started a home accounting business, so when he was let go he focused on this new endeavor. Starting a business is hard work, especially with no extra capital. But by God's grace we continued to move forward, confident that it was His will for families to be together and live in the country.

At times our search for a more secluded area was discouraging. Real estate was escalating in price. We would find an area that we liked and watch prices double right before our eyes! During our search we also implemented changes in our home life. We decided to try to start living as if we were already in the country; we stayed at home much more often, developed a schedule, studied more, sought the company of those in whom we perceived a desire to prepare for heaven, and simplified our lives by having four garage sales.

True Education

While attending Family Camp meeting in our state, I drove up with a friend to visit a nearby ministry. Their property was beautiful. It overlooked a valley with a breathtaking view of the surrounding mountains. I looked at my friend and said, "This is nice. I could live here!" We had a wonderful time of fellowship and learning. Life was brightened by a clearer vision of what country life could mean.

We began to feel displaced; were out of place in the city, but could find no country home. This was not an easy time, especially when we assumed the deeper responsibility for what our children would see and hear. Certain practices in our church seemed more and more out of place. We were disturbed by the type of music we were hearing, the drama presented during the worship service, the videos shown for church, and erroneous sermons. There were materials being used in the children's department that did not appear to be "thoroughly winnowed."

Unless the student has pure mental food, thoroughly winnowed from the so-called 'higher education,' which is mingled with infidel sentiments, he cannot truly know God. Only those who cooperate with heaven in the plan of salvation can know what true education in its simplicity means. Those who seek the education that the world esteems so highly are gradually led farther and farther from the principles of truth, until they become educated worldlings. At what a price have they gained their education! (Counsels to Teachers, page 15).

"Should we be exposing Rachel to this type of church service, Buck?" I would quietly ask my husband after yet another "entertaining" Sabbath School.

It seemed there was always a ready answer with a reference we had just read such as, *Not one jot or tittle of anything theatrical should be brought into our work* (*Evangelism*, 137).

We finally decided to conduct Sabbath school at home and then attend church for the sermon hour. But as our convictions increased, we felt we had to withdraw, but were reticent to totally forsake the "assembling together." What should we do?

We prayed and asked the Lord to lead us to like believers. We didn't want to change church families only to change again when we moved, but we concluded, after much prayer, that any inconvenience would be worth finding truth. We prayed about and "discovered" (not by accident!) a wonderful group of people who met on Sabbath afternoons to watch a prophecy series on end time events. Meeting with these committed believers was like water to our thirsty souls.

The Property

We found properties online that had the criterion that we were looking for—a top ten list—privacy, beauty, southern exposure, at least 20 acres, within our price range, a spring, plenty of trees, and agricultural land that could be tilled for a garden. (If we had to do it again we would have thought a little more about access. But everything is a learning experience! If you live in an area with lots of snow, and you have to get in and out, your road and/or driveway needs to be level enough to allow for that. If you have ice and a steep road, there can be problems.)

We obtained catalogues that listed land for sale in the area in which we desired to locate. After selecting several properties that met our needs we contacted a realtor. We spent a long, unrewarding day viewing several undesirable settings. Then we came to the last piece: 20 acres of good land, several springs, a beautiful stand of pines, a south-facing meadow for a home site and garden. We felt the Lord leading us to this place. Buck and I made an offer on this piece of land and prayed.

The Prayer

Upon arriving back at our suburban home we made a list of things that would need to happen in order for us to be able to make the move. Some of the items on our list included: 1) obtaining financing in order to buy the property until our home sold, 2) make improvements on our house to make it more marketable, and 3) that Buck would be able to take his client base with him across the state. We worked with renewed vigor to get the house ready to sell, and we prayed some more. We prayed for God's will, that if His desire was for us to move to this location, the house would sell and that we could come to an acceptable price on the land. We also researched how much the current owner of the property paid for the land. We found out that we had bid too low. The price he paid was more than we thought. He came back with a higher counter offer. It was within an acceptable range so we accepted.

At last our house was ready to sell. Wanting to get as much equity as possible, we tried selling it ourselves. It was a seller's market at the time—the height of the real estate bubble. We knew it would burst at some point, and became more and more anxious as the weeks went by when no one inquired about our house! We then listed it with a do-it-yourself listing agency. We had prayed that the Lord would bring us a seller so that the selling commission could be used to put into our new home. The day we put the new sign in the yard a young man walked by and said that he liked our house and may be interested in buying it. He lived on the next street with his parents. He was marrying soon and wanted to live near them. He soon returned with his father and the four of us sat around the kitchen table and negotiated the contract. The whole transaction was a very pleasant experience.

Now we had raw land, but no dwelling in which to live. We thought about buying a travel trailer and living in that while we built a home, but we really didn't want to tie up so much money. We made some calls and networked with a church member in the area who put us in touch with a family in his church that could rent us a cabin. We moved into the cabin the end of July 2006. About all that was accomplished that first year was building the access road. The next year the building site was excavated and the basement walls poured. Then the basement floor was poured, the walls framed, and a floor constructed. A log home builder put up the log walls.

Being your own contractor is hard work: overseeing the logging, peeling of the logs, and certain aspects of roofing the house. That December, we went on a business trip to Seattle and left the finishing of the roof in the hands of our builder, George, but with the roof only half finished, he phoned us with the news that he had broken his leg! Buck and I had prayed for months for the Lord to hold back the snow, "... just until we can get the roof on." And now it was so close! As if He could hold it back no longer, our area received a whole year's accumulation and within days there was 2 feet of snow in half of our house! Discouraged? We were tempted, but hadn't the Lord seen us through this far? He wouldn't leave us now.

A cat plowed our road so that we could get to the house. My husband hired another builder and the two of them shoveled all of the snow out of the house, nailed the plywood on the roof, and tacked a tarp on it. Finally, it was set for winter.

The following summer we finished the roof. George, our original builder, had squeezed us into his schedule, though he had an obligation to build another house and was still healing from his broken leg. We had limited funds. Could we find another contractor? There was no one was like George! I felt my doubts beginning to overpower my trust in God's leading, but I placed my worries at the foot of the cross. It was the least sacrifice I could do for Him after all he had done for me!

Lessons in Waiting

The Lord has taught me so much. I now know that He wants to be my teacher and my counselor moment by moment. The problem is that I have been taught by the world's methods for so long, it's hard for me to listen for His voice. Satan is always there to distract me or suggest causes for doubt. When I am tempted to doubt I remind myself, "Here is the patience of the saints: here are they that keep the commandments of God, and the faith of Jesus." Rev 14:12. It is my desire to have the kind of patience that will see me through the end times. God, in His mercy, is giving me opportunities to develop that patience!

So where are we now? Have we arrived? Not quite. As for the house, we are just finishing the plumbing as we write this. We are still waiting for George to install the windows and doors. "I'm almost finished on the other house," he told us just the other day. "I want to help you guys get into your house." What a blessing that will be!

With the majority of our belongings in storage while living in the small cabin, and always needing what I didn't have, I wondered if our new house would ever get finished. I wanted "my stuff," but, even more importantly, I needed to learn about letting God be in control. I wanted a nice home. I wanted to be in a home *this year*. I didn't want to wait another winter.

My husband was busy full time with his accounting business, so I decided to work on the house myself. Every day I would take the children out to the property (they were then 5 and 8 years of age) and work on the plumbing. But, as I worked on the house, I was strongly impressed that God had called me to work with and train my children. I realized that I was allowing the house to become a distraction from my "first" work. I felt that I couldn't focus on the house and get things done as quickly as I wanted, and still give the necessary attention the children needed in their home schooling program. Working on the house was my own agenda.

Through the process of trial and error, I have learned that God knows my weaknesses and what is best for my own character development. I thank Him for His patience with me and for the opportunity to learn and grow. He has given me opportunities to surrender and to let go of my way of doing things. In the process, I have an opportunity let go of the pride that clings tenaciously to my own selfish will. It is more important to get *me* done than to get "my" house finished!

Country School Blessings

By moving to the country, our family has learned so much—not necessarily the skills that I would have considered valuable five years ago when we lived in the city, though. I realize, now, that they are skills and knowledge that God desired for us to learn. The key to true happiness is surrender; the surrender of my deepest hopes and wildest dreams, even the sorrow of broken dreams. But, He does not just want me to accept, of necessity, the mere surrender of my own will and ideas, He desires me to have the ability to rejoice in my daily lesson in the School of Christ.

One of the blessings that has come from living in the country is applying God's method of learning with practical lessons from the garden, nature, and quiet times of worship. There is so much more to learning when I choose to be enrolled in the school of Christ. God's first classroom was with the first family in the Garden of Eden. It is vital to use the Bible as our school textbook in order to discover the true "higher" education.

I now ask God each morning, "Lord, what do you want to teach me today?" I know that if my family and I continue to ask that question daily, we will be enrolling in that school from which we will never graduate.

This world is the school in which we are to prepare for graduation into the higher school (*Special Testimonies*, Series B, No. 7. p. 45). I want to keep my mind open to the eternal truths of infinite wisdom that only God can give so that I can help direct my family toward heaven. The crown of immortal glory is worth every sacrifice.

By faith we may stand on the threshold of the eternal city, and hear the gracious welcome given to those who in this life cooperate with Christ, regarding it as an honor to suffer for His sake. As the words are spoken, 'Come, ye blessed of My Father,' they cast their crowns at the feet of the Redeemer, exclaiming, 'Worthy is the Lamb that was slain to receive power, and riches, and wisdom, and strength, and honor, and glory, and blessing. . . . Honor, and glory, and power, be unto Him that sitteth upon the throne, and unto the Lamb for ever and ever' (Matthew 25:34; Revelation 5:12, 13, *Acts of the Apostles*, p. 601).

C H A P T E R

FIFTEEN

Country Living Miracle

SANDIA WALLER

But my God shall supply all your need
according to his riches in glory by Christ Jesus.
Philippians 4:19

Ray and Sandia had become more and more uncomfortable in their neigh-
borhood. When the neighbor kicked their door in, they knew that it was no
longer safe for themselves or their children to live in the strife and confusion
of the city. Sandia began to dream of the home they would one day have;
there would be a large picture window through which she would see acres
of rolling farmland and pine trees, "where the deer and the antelope play."
But, really, what could they do? They had no money saved. How would the
Lord get them out? They might as well ask for a trip to the moon!

It was our 10th wedding anniversary. My husband, Ray, and I decided to treat ourselves to a ten day camp meeting—one day for each year of marriage. Our sense of nostalgia ran high, but only until we discovered there was no such thing as a ten day long camp meeting these days. Camp meetings are often a one-day workshop where you bring your own lunch.

We were still sold on the idea of celebrating a ten day camp meeting, however, so we decided to travel out of state, if necessary, for a full stay. Eight hours away, at a place in Oklahoma called Tenfold Advantage Family Camp, at the Conference Campground, Wewoka Woods, we found what we were looking for. We were thrilled.

From swimming, to canoeing, to action-packed children's meetings, we had a blast. Our horseback ride reminded us of the horseback riding we did on our honeymoon. The highlight for us was listening to the speaker for the event, Jere Franklin, from Canada. When we read the itinerary and saw the aggressive topics he would cover (Mark of the Beast, The Time of No Buy-No Sell, etc.), we braced ourselves for a conspiracy discussion, but he focused on the high-lights of the overall message of preparedness. Instead, our hearts were warmed at every message; he told endearing stories of his uncle, the love of God, and the importance of heart preparation. Practical classes included country living skills like cutting timber, building log cabins, making soap, digging wells, making bread and home made gluten! We were charmed.

Just a few months earlier, we had listened to a presentation at our Hous-ton church done by Mountain Media Ministries. They admonished us of the wonderful benefits of living in the country versus crowded city living. We were more than ready for a change, but it would get worse before we escaped!

Desire Fed by Appetite

Reading the Bible and the booklet, *Country Living*, by Ellen White, our desire for a quiet home in the country increased daily. God had been gracious in providing for us while in Houston, yet we knew this could only be temporary if we were going to have the best spiritual advantage. Our children were being negatively influenced by their surroundings. We had to do something—but what? Our options appeared severely limited.

We passed the remainder of the year reading and wondering how to reconcile reality with our ever-increasing desire for a country home. New Year's Day rolled around with no change for the better; against the backdrop of Houston's 4-million person rush hour traffic, we were still sidestepping across sidewalks littered with broken beer bottles and canine calling cards, foul-mouthed neighbors and half-clad fitness club members. That evening, January 1, 2012, we topped our prayer list with the following request:

"Please give us a home in the country." Sounds simple enough right? But we had some dreams attending the request. We wanted this home to have a million-dollar view (with no million dollars in pocket to secure such a request), no close neighbors (yet 20 minutes from town), bedrooms for each child, and the opportunity to walk to work, church, school, and the store. The only place we could think of that would somewhat match this was if we were to live in walking distance of a college campus which technically would not satisfy the item about "no close neighbors". It was obvious that our dream home did not exist, but we kept praying, anyway.

The Day It Happened

March rolled around. By this time, the neighborhood children had taken to beating on our front door and windows, demanding that we let them in. Once, while we were eating lunch in the dining room, the door banging began in earnest. Suddenly, our locked front door was kicked in by the neighbor who was offended that we did not respond to his demands. We sat there stunned. The neighbor just stood outside on our porch, smiling with pleasure at our obvious astonishment. After this episode, our prayers became more desperate.

Lord, we must get out of this city. You have promised, in Medical Ministry 310, that you would help your people "find such homes outside the cities." Please, show us the way. Do whatever you have to do to get us out.

That's when it happened. My husband and I were sitting at the park watching our children play, and speaking to each other about our nor-

mal daily activities. After a short silence, my husband said something that did not fit into the flow of our conversation.

"The Lord just told me I would be leading a lifestyle center."

I laughed. He didn't return the laugh. I tried to sober up. When we reached home, I began checking out lifestyle center websites. In our search, we discovered that in three weeks Neil Nedley was scheduled to speak in Dallas, Texas. My husband signed up to attend the series. Ray's thinking was that since Dr. Nedley was president of a lifestyle center, maybe he would be fortunate enough to talk with him or even submit a résumé.

Sobriety Test

While my Ray was busy signing up for the seminar, I was reminded of a conversation we had with two friends several years ago, greatly extolling the virtues of a lifestyle center called Black Hills. With this reminder fresh in mind, we checked Black Hills out on the web. To our complete shock, there was an opening listed for President/CEO!

Amazing! We made a phone call and Ray submitted his résumé. This seemed so outrageously unbelievable to us that we wondered if we should even bother. We might as well have been saying something like this:

Husband: "You know, honey, I've always wanted to travel to the moon."

Wife: "Oh, that's wonderful! You should contact NASA, dear. Maybe you can get in on their next space mission."

Husband: "Great idea, I'll call them today."

Wife: "Perfect! Perhaps they'll get back to us in time to see Mars?"

Husband: "This is all so exciting!"

Wonder of wonders, Black Hills *did* call us! The next thing we knew we *were* on a flight! Not to the moon, though. We were flying to South Dakota, at the invitation of the Black Hills Health and Education Center. The campus was nestled on 250 acres of gorgeous rolling valleys, red clay hills, and bubbling creeks. We enthusiastically partook of the delicious plant-based food, enjoyed warm church fellowship with like-minded believers, inspected the well-stocked store, and visited the school that our children would attend. As I stood in awe, looking around me, I suddenly realized that everything we needed would all be within walking distance, that is, *if* we were invited to come.

Puzzling Answer

The icing on the cake came when we toured the home that was being provided for the incoming president. Every window held a panoramic, million dollar view! We were speechless. Our tour guide asked, "If you folks ended up here in this capacity, would this house be adequate for your needs?" We assured him it would be! Each of our children would have their own bedroom.

The whole weekend, including surprise interviews with staff, and un-expected meetings with the executive board chair and committee members, was a delight. We even got to see Mount Rushmore which was just 20 minutes away!

Back in Houston, we excitedly thanked our friends for the encouraging testimony they gave us about Black Hills, and that it was looking favorable to our moving there.

"Congratulations! God is good!" They said. "But, honestly, we have never heard of Black Hills. The place we told you about was called Hartland."

Ray and I just looked at each other with our mouths open! For several days, we remained puzzled as to how the name Black Hills had come into our minds. We had no other frame of reference except what we thought our friends had told us. A few days later a little light was shed on the mystery when we emptied out our bag of conference collectibles from a recent GYC Conference that we had attended in Houston. Among the literature we had collected, we discovered a Black Hills brochure. Just about then, we received word that we were hired, and the Black Hills brochure actually helped us prepare for our move. It was almost as if God was dropping us little pieces of puzzle, on a need to know basis. Did He have this all planned? Was He just waiting for us to get serious? The picture came together with a rush. In no time at all, we had a country home.

That's how we came to live "where the deer and the antelope play"—literally. We have encountered everything from wild buffalo to mountain lions, from wild burros to white tailed deer. It's still too exciting to think of as commonplace. Life is beautiful, from every window in our home.

Full Circle

The joy of this astounding experience just keeps expanding. In August of 2012, at ASI Convention in Ohio, our Black Hills booth was located just around the corner from the *You Can Survive!* booth where Jere and Linda Franklin were again spreading the word about God's call to country living. It was exactly one year earlier that we had heard their message promoting the benefits of country life, assuring those of us in the audience that God is faithful to do exceedingly, abundantly, above all that we could ever ask or think! Well, I'm here to affirm that this is absolutely true!

Regardless of what lies ahead, we have experienced the hand of God around and under us. I have no doubt that He is ready to open a way of escape for every family who allows Him to plant the love of country in their heart!

SIXTEEN

My Way or His Way?

CYNTHIA MILLER

*Now unto Him that is able to do exceeding abundantly
above all that we ask or think, according to the power that
worketh in us, unto Him be glory in the church by Christ Jesus
throughout all ages, world without end. Amen.*
Eph. 3:20, 21

*When we met Alan Miller at our YCS seminar in West Virginia a few years
ago, something he said about parrots caught my attention. I love collecting
bird stories*, so I listened intently when he told me a fascinating story of
how one of their young Yellow-nape Amazon youngsters had adopted a lady
in a wheelchair. I had no idea where Alan and Cynthia were in their spiritual journey, but when I received an update on their move to the country,
I knew their story had to be told.*

**On a Wing and a Prayer* by Linda Franklin is available through Amazon, or ruth@youcansur-
vive.org.

"I will never give up my parrots!" I had made that proclamation more than once. I was absolutely devoted to my birds; caring for the breeding pairs, feeding them twice daily, hand-feeding their babies every 2 to 3 hours, and cleaning aviaries and cages. My husband and children questioned before they ate any of the fresh fruits and vegetables in the refrigerator, "Are these ours, or are they for the birds?"

Paradise Interrupted

Living in South Florida with my birds seemed like paradise—until September 11, 2001. On that very day, my priorities were altered, for I knew that our world had forever changed. The Holy Spirit started urging me with the thought of leaving the city for country living. I knew what the Spirit of Prophecy said in regard to leaving the cities, but I had parrots! My life had been just fine until this event happened. Relocating to a remote location did not fit into my plans. I decided to keep my thoughts about this move to myself, partly in hopes that these convictions might just go away, but they didn't.

My love for parrots did not coincide with living in a country setting in the mountains, where I was pretty sure God's plan would lead. I decided to start praying for my heart to change about this love for parrots. At that time, we had over 60 birds, and I loved each one as if they were my own children. How could I give them up? I needed Jesus to change my heart, to love Him and obey His ways more than loving the parrots. I was at a "Y" in the road; was it to be my way or His way?

I willingly prayed, "Jesus, please remove my love for these beautiful birds and help me to find good homes for them. I only want to do Your will. I want to live where You want me to live." I was convinced of the Holy Spirit's leading at this point.

It is a mystery how He accomplished it, but the Lord did work a miracle—He changed my heart! I finally told my husband of my impression that we should find a country home and sell the birds. He knew that I had "turned a page" as far as the parrots were concerned and that I was serious about living in the country.

The Challenge

But how would we purchase a country property? We didn't have any savings, for all spare monies went to the upkeep of the parrot business, but I knew that if it was absolutely God's leading, that He would provide a way. God has always been faithful to us whenever we placed our hands in His.

Years ago, The Lord sent us to Kentucky, right out of college, to do dark county work. We started our little family in the Kentucky hills. After having our first child, we discovered, a year later, that we were expecting twins! Unfortunately, they were not full term when they entered this world. Needless to say, hospital and doctor bills were enormous, and we had no insurance. We were self-supporting and lived on very little income. There were very few jobs available. When my husband asked me if I thought the Lord would ever send us back to Kentucky, I verbalized a quick, "I don't think so!"

Now, considering the purchase of country property, we looked at listings in a few states and discovered, ironically, that Kentucky had the cheapest land prices. Kentucky was not at the top of my list, but I smiled as I thought to myself, "He is going to send us back."

I vividly recall that it was exactly 12 noon the day my husband called one particular Kentucky realtor. Alan told the woman who answered the phone what we were looking for and she proceeded to tell us what she had listed. Nothing she read to us met our "country criteria" list. Then she told us that she owned a piece of land that was not on the market, but that she was willing to sell it. As she described her own property, it sounded exactly like what we were looking for, but even more than we had dared to dream about! What were the chances that this person would be there at lunch time and answer the phone? We knew that this was God's providence!

We made arrangements to make the trip to see this piece. Since it was at the busiest time of year at the citrus company where I worked as the main supervisor, and because I had the parrots to care for, Alan made the trip from Florida to Kentucky without me. When he arrived, the realtor's husband made it clear to Alan that he did not what to sell the property, but he showed it to him anyway. Alan has never met a stranger, so by the time these two men had walked those beautiful 400 acres, the owner's heart was changed.

"I like you!" he said to Alan. "I'll sell my place to you."

When Alan returned and described the property, I recognized that it was exactly what we needed: it was entirely self-sufficient, we could grow a nice garden, and there was plenty of water and trees, even free natural gas! Things were happening so fast that I changed my prayer.

"Lord, if this isn't the place we are to buy, then, somehow, stop the sale." He did not stop the sale. In less than three months, the deal was closed. We had a place in the country, but we still had the parrots!

He Is Able

Advertising the birds began in earnest. How would I feel seeing them go to their new homes? I did cry a few tears when I sold my favorite ones, but I knew I was doing the right thing. The Lord did change the desires of my heart—away from the birds to a whole new way of living. I have never regretted my decision. I can think back on the birds fondly, but that sentimental, emotional bond is gone. Only God could have done that for me!

Our property? He provided far more than we asked. He is able! Alan and I feel a little like the picture we read in Exodus of Moses going to the wilderness to unlearn and relearn life's lessons according to God's ways. We work hard, but being away from the city bustle and the city's rat race, living in a country setting where there is peace and quiet, is the most wonderful way to live.

God sent us back to Kentucky, to a dark county, to spread the everlasting gospel with folks who have not yet heard the good news of the Three Angel's Message. True, a parrot is a lifetime investment, but somehow investing in eternity seems much more worthwhile!

C H A P T E R

SEVENTEEN

"Go For It!"

JOHN ERICKSON

For I know the thoughts that I think toward you, saith the LORD,
thoughts of peace, and not of evil, to give you an expected end.
Jeremiah 29:11

A few months after we met John at a camp meeting in Minnesota, he sent us a letter of thanks that included these remarks: "I do not wish to flatter you, for we are counseled not to do so, but I wanted to let you know that God has used you to make a difference in my life. You wondered, aloud at the camp meeting, whether the people would actually implement the counsel we have been given. God used you to make all the difference in the world to me. Thanks for everything you and your wife have taught me, but most of all, for being willing to be used to motivate me to do the right thing and to help me understand this important topic (country living)."

225

"Lord, you know I want to follow your will in this area more than anybody. Please help me to get out into the country and follow the counsel we have been given."

Hi, my name is John, I'm 25 years old, and this is my story of how God cleared the way for me to experience country living.

Unexpected Changes

A little over a year ago, I went through the heart-breaking experience of a broken engagement. As I battled through this trying time, the Lord began to make unexpected changes in my life. One of those changes involved country living. Soon after the breakup, I began to feel like I needed to discover what God really expected of me in the area of country living. I had many questions, and it was difficult to know where to start. I felt like I needed a nudge in the right direction—someone to show me the ropes.

My golden opportunity came in the form of a handbill advertising a camp meeting in Middle River, Minnesota during the summer of 2012. I immediately knew that I wanted to go to hear Jere Franklin speak about this subject.

The subject of country living came alive as Jere spoke. My questions began to be answered. Perplexities started to vanish. A whole new way of life opened to my view. What impressed me the most was not the practical demonstrations of old fashioned skills, but rather the spiritual approach Jere took to the subject. He wasn't a crackpot, a sensationalist, fanatic, or heretic, but an ordinary man who allowed himself to be used by God to preach about the lifestyle God desires for His people in these last days.

Transformation

I've always disliked camping, found learning about outdoor skills to be boring, and have been much more interested in computers than compost. Let's just say that God has transformed my thinking. For the first time in my life, I understood more fully the Enoch model for ministry and wanted to set up an outpost center of my own. The implications of the time of no-buy-no-sell went from being theoretical to practical.

As the meetings drew to a close, I still didn't know how or when I would be able to make my way out into the country, but I made it a matter of prayer and decided to take steps to position myself for the change. I might not be able to immediately get out of town, but there were many activities I could pursue to help myself to make the transition. I began to learn skills such as fire starting, ax craft, food storage, gardening, using knives and machetes, wilderness survival techniques, and too many other skills to mention. I ordered fruit bushes, open-pollinated seeds, and began reading the Spirit of Prophecy and other books to further educate myself.

The search for a way out began. How could I "bust out" of the city? I knew that we are told not to make any rash moves in this area, so I kept praying that I wouldn't go ahead of God's plan or lag behind it. I also knew that the solution wasn't likely to just fall out of the sky into my lap, I well knew the counsel stating that many of God's people will have to work hard to open up the way. I determined to do my part. I had land, with a well and wood available, at no cost to myself. Housing became my main concern.

I scoured the Internet for housing solutions. I looked at everything from stick-built, modular, manufactured, dome homes, yurts, shipping containers, cob homes, square bale houses, structurally insulated panels, and everything in between. Everything was just too expensive and I didn't want to go deep into debt. A thirty-year mortgage in a self-imposed debt prison (an expensive house) did not seem like the right thing to do. Finally, after countless hours spent in research, I decided to buy a fairly inexpensive 504 sq. foot cabin. God has provided the way for me to obtain private financing and to be able to pay it off in 1-2 years as opposed to 20 years.

The Enoch Walk

I am truly excited at what the Lord has in store for me and all who will be blessed by my own little outpost center in rural North Dakota. I'm looking forward to learning how to have that deeper walk with God that Enoch enjoyed.

To those who are on the fence regarding country living—I say, "Go for it!" When you do your part, the Lord will do His part. Be faithful to the light that you have and the Lord will show you the next step. Be willing to be humble—to set aside your preconceived ideas and to find out the awesome plan God has for you, your family, and those who will be blessed by your obedience.

EIGHTEEN

Our Country Living Story

ROBIN AND BONNIE ROGERS

But without faith it is impossible to please him:
for he that cometh to God must believe that he is,
and that he is a rewarder of them that diligently seek Him.

Hebrews 11:6

Robin and Bonnie were sure they wanted to raise Rachel in the country. They had no idea the lessons God had in store for them to learn! Though it sometimes looked as if they had made mistakes, more than once God was just upgrading their plans. He had an even better plan; He wanted them to learn to listen to His still, small voice on their way to paradise.

Phase One

The beginning of our journey toward country living began shortly after we (Robin and Bonnie) were married in 1998. We were living in Apopka, Florida (a suburban area outside of Orlando) in a home that Robin owned before we were married. We both understood the counsel for country living and knew this was also the best environment for Rachel (my then eleven-year-old daughter from a previous marriage). Rachel had spent the first seven-and-one-half years of her life in rural Minnesota, and I had so much longed to be back in a country environment. So, our home was put on the market almost immediately after our marriage and we began praying for God's guidance and direction.

Robin was a piano technician for a piano company in the Orlando area (his first job) and also a paid organist for a Lutheran church (his second job), so he knew that moving into a country environment meant that he would most probably have to pursue self-employment in his trade. That was a leap of faith for him. I was not working, having recently quit her job as an accounting clerk in another city, in order to marry and relocate to Apopka.

We also knew that in order to make country living work for us that we could only purchase a home within our means and without a mortgage. Fortunately, with God's blessing and frugality, we both had accumulated small nest eggs while we were single. Fortunately, neither of us were in debt when we married. That was a huge blessing for us as a family.

Within five months after listing it, we had a buyer for our home! However, we had no idea where we were to go. My mother and step-father also lived in Florida. When we called them, they suggested we consider Murphy, North Carolina where they had just recently purchased a second home as a summer home, in the mountains of western North Carolina. They suggested that we take a week to drive up and check it out. My mother had already done a little asking around for us and was told that there was need of a piano technician in the area. We prayed and decided that was a good plan, and asked God to confirm whether there would, indeed, be work for him in this area or not.

When we arrived in Murphy, the first thing we did was to contact the Chamber of Commerce in this little rural mountain town. We figured they would know the prospects of self-employment for Robin in his profession. Well, the lady-in-charge practically begged us to come! She indicated, most positively, that there was need of a piano technician in this area, so, God confirmed Phase I of our journey! Murphy was the place!

Phase Two

Now, we needed to see if there was anything in the way of decent affordable housing available for us with at least some of the criteria for which we were looking. The realtor that my folks had used was not available to work with us due to emergency personal matters that came up. However, after praying, we felt that the one God impressed us to contact was just the right one. She led us to several properties, some of which were cutting it really close with our budget. But, the last one she showed us was the one that both us said after we saw it: "This is it!" It was a small, log-sided cabin on the top of a hill, off a long winding, rural paved road: about 900 square feet with two bedrooms, one-and-one-half baths, an unfinished basement of about 200 square feet, and a single car garage. The down side was that it was only 1.21 acres, but it did have a small garden space that we could develop. Plus, it had a well. There was vacant land on one side of us and a neighbor on the other side, yet we were secluded from view, due to the forest that separated the neighbor from us on one side and the vacant land on the other. And, best of all, it was within our budget.

Between the two of us, we had just enough money to purchase this home, and with what we would net from the sale of our home in Florida, we would be able to purchase this little cabin as a cash sale! The total price was $51,000. We even had a little left over for our small savings account. We were thrilled! Our prayers/dreams were being answered! Our new little home was about a half hour from My mother and stepfather's summer home was located.

Digging In

Six weeks later, we arrived at our new home, and began in earnest to prepare as we knew the Lord would have us do. Robin soon made the acquaintance of a man who had a piano sales business that he operated

out of his home. This turned out to be a very good business relationship, as this gentleman provided many referrals to Robin for piano tuning. Additionally, he providentially got to know the owner of a discount herb and vitamin store in a nearby town who kindly told him that he "knew everybody in town" and could provide him with as much business as he wanted! That turned out to be a very true statement! Robin also sent out letters, with his business card, to all of the churches in the Tri-State area (western North Carolina, North Georgia, and eastern Tennessee) introducing himself as the Tri-State area's new piano technician.

Within a week, he began getting his first calls. His business grew as word-of-mouth advertising spread. Soon he began getting residential calls as well. The Lord greatly blessed and Robin has not had to advertise as do most businesses. His reputation of quality and dependable service follows him from place to place, and church to church. In the second month after our arrival in Murphy, God also provided Robin's second job as a paid church organist for a Presbyterian church. God was providing for us and we were thrilled!!

The garden plot was quite rocky and Robin had his work cut out for him in making raised beds in which to plant. But, with a lot of hard work and effort, we did manage to grow a small variety of crops, including a grape vine. Growing much of our own food helped cut down on our grocery bill.

It was also at this little cabin that I began to learn the art of canning. I had previously been shown by a friend how to preserve food, and with God's blessing Rachel and I were soon canning many jars of applesauce from apples we purchased from one of the orchards in the area.

Reaching Out

We have quite enjoyed this change from city to country living in this quaint little rural mountain town. It is quite easy to make friends, and most everyone will wave as they pass us on the highway or on the street. We quickly got to know most of our neighbors and were able to share our faith as the Lord gave opportunities. We made our own opportunities as well with bulk mailings of present truth literature to our rural route area. We gave homemade bread to our neighbors along w/ a piece of present truth literature at Christmastime. We also went to large religious gatherings in Atlanta, Charlotte, Chattanooga, and Knoxville to distribute present truth literature. Most of these cities are within a two-hour drive from our home. Rachel thrived in this country setting and we were all at peace.

Deliverance from Embarrassment and Difficulty

One incident after we became comfortable in our new surroundings is worth sharing, for the sake of those who may be remodeling an older home. Seek the Lord's will first; it may save you money, time, and embarrassment! Winter would soon be coming and we needed new windows in our cabin. My mother had agreed to loan us the money to get them. We were going to have Home Depot install them. As soon as we had signed the contract and phoned in the credit card information from my mother's credit card, we left for camp meeting. Brother Jere Franklin was one of the speakers there and spoke about not being in debt or going in debt. Up to this point in our pursuit of a country home, we had not gone into debt. However, we had reasoned that it was okay since we were just getting a loan from my mother instead of a bank. However, conviction set in; we had made a grand mistake once we heard Brother Franklin speak on the topic of debt. He confirmed what we already knew, but had not

obeyed! We should have trusted God for his timing and finances in getting those windows.

So, now we were thinking "What are we going to do? How can we extricate ourselves from this problem, or can we?" I remembered that Brother Franklin quoted a promise from *The Desire of Ages*, page 329:

> *Whatever your anxieties and trials, spread out your case before the Lord. Your spirit will be braced for endurance. The way will be opened for you to disentangle yourself from embarrassment and difficulty.*

Aha! We knew we needed to pray. We claimed that promise immediately. God worked a miracle and did just what He had promised!

Soon after we arrived home from camp meeting, we received a phone call from Home Depot telling us that something was apparently wrong with the credit card number we had given them. It wasn't working!!

They had tried to run it through their system more than once, but it would not work. They verified the number with us and then asked if we would like to put it on a Home Depot credit card instead.

"No...if the credit card number doesn't work, we will not be able to purchase the windows."

"Okay," said the kind man. And that was the end of our "inescapable dilemma." We thought they might try to hold us to the contract and possibly take us to court, but they didn't! We were elated! God is faithful to get us out of jams when we stupidly do things He would not have us do, but he likes us to "reason together"… first!

My mother was quite upset when she found out that Home Depot couldn't get her credit card to work. She kept insisting that her credit was impeccable and that this had never happened to her before!

"All is well, Mom," I assured her. "Really, it's okay! God overruled your perfect credit-rating in order to answer our prayers. You see, Mom, we had decided, while at camp meeting, that we did not want to be in debt to anyone, even you, because debt was not God's will, but we didn't know how to get out of our contract with Home Depot!"

My mother was concerned about our being ready for winter, but God was taking care of, that, too. A few months later, when we had saved enough money to purchase new windows, we found a company that would do the job for less than half the price that we would have paid through Home Depot! Isn't God good? He taught us a valuable lesson, and prevented us from making a costly mistake. We were always so thankful that we were in the right place at the right time (camp meeting) to hear Brother Franklin speak on the topic of debt. Our hearts were re-convicted. God rewarded our faith as we claimed His promise, and acted on it, accordingly.

Things don't always turn out that well, though. After we'd lived in our little cabin for five years, we were tempted to make a similar mistake. After trying to grow a garden for a few years, we realized the need for a lot more land, for gardening than what we had. We had looked at quite a number of different properties in our area hoping to find a suitable place with more acreage. However, we had not been successful in finding anything within our budget. While in Kentucky at a camp meeting we heard of a rural area not too far away from where the camp meeting was being held that had some new homes for sale.

My impulsiveness got the better of me, and after the camp meeting it was arranged for us to take a look at some of these homes. Lo and behold, before we had headed back home to North Carolina, we had both signed on the dotted line (with a down payment of $1000) to purchase one of these homes! Some would call it "buyer's remorse," but reality set in later. We knew that we did not have a clear "go-ahead" from the Lord. Both of us became quite uneasy about our commitment. Nevertheless, we put our little cabin up for sale, with a realtor, and waited. Because of our uneasiness, though, we also sought the Lord and asked him to block the sale of our home in Murphy if it was not his will for us to move to Kentucky.

Through a providential array of circumstances, the Lord made it undeniably clear that we had moved out ahead of him. Confirmation came when God did indeed block the sale of our home during our six-month contract. We had many potential buyers that came to look at our home, but, none of them even ventured a contract of any kind, for various reasons. We did lose the $1,000, but it taught me a valuable lesson in not running ahead of the Lord, especially when Robin had reservations about purchasing that home in Kentucky and wasn't really in favor it. After that, we just put our little country cabin "on the altar" and asked God to orchestrate our future moves, *according to His will.*

God's Plans Are Best

Well, we need not have been concerned about our future whereabouts and how we would ever be able to have that extra garden acreage we needed. God had been preparing our future dwelling place all along before we had even married!

As you recall from the beginning of our story, my mother and stepfather had purchased a mountain home in Murphy, a few weeks before we were married (six months before we purchased our little cabin). They were both seventy-two-years-old at the time. The home they purchased was a large home on five-and-one-half acres; including some significant wooded area. It was their spring/summer get-away from the heat of Florida. They had been coming up each year during the spring and would stay until early October. Their hobby was horticulture; fruit and vegetable gardening, as well as flowers. There was no landscaping, garden, and very few plants to speak of when they purchased it. They spent literally almost all of their waking hours outside preparing a vegetable garden site, developing a small orchard area, and landscaping the rest of the property with a variety of beautiful flowering trees, bushes, colorful annual flowers and perennials. Since the home sits at the top of a hill, the majority of the landscaping was done in large tiered sections with moss-covered walkways between the three tiers secured by landscape timbers with little concrete benches on each tier to sit and enjoy the beauty on each level. It is indeed a majestic and scenic area of the property.

In addition, my step-father created walking trails in the wooded area behind the property, including a rustic wooden bridge and a campfire pit. Amidst these restful forest walking trails, was a bench here and there where one could sit and rest and enjoy the beauty of these natural surroundings. My step-father suffered a stroke which left him with some partial paralysis. However, he desired to get his rehabilitation from the stroke naturally by doing the landscape work on the above-mentioned three-tiered area. Although there are some neighbors, the way that the house is situated and landscaped provides plenty of privacy.

My stepfather was diagnosed with cancer and passed away about a year later; just a couple of months past his eightieth birthday in March, 2006. By this time, he and my mother had prepared a virtual "country paradise" but he never really got to fully enjoy all of it before he passed away. We remember him saying on his death bed that though he wouldn't be around to enjoy it, that someone else would. A memorial marker and cremation ashes were put at the exact location he specified before he passed away—under a favorite tree with a beautiful array of ferns and other foliage surrounding it.

Phase Three

About three months later, my mother asked to have a little meeting with us. We were not prepared for her suggestion.

"How would you like to sell your little cabin and move into her summer mountain home as "caretakers" with no rent or cost?" She also offered to pay all maintenance costs associated with the property, and to pay the property taxes and homeowner's insurance as well. (If she had not offered to do that, there would have been no way we would have been able to afford to live there.) By this time, she had realized that she could not properly care for this home by herself nor did she want to spend an entire spring and summer there alone.)

By this time, we knew better than to say yes without consulting the Lord. We'd had two unforgettable lessons in that regard! We prayed earnestly and sought counsel, both from the Bible and the Spirit of Prophecy, as well as from very committed and spiritually dedicated brethren who knew us well. We made a list of advantages and disadvantages that would be associated with making this move. In the end, the advantages definitely outweighed the disadvantages. We really didn't want a home this large, but it seemed that this was the way that God was directing. Not wanting to make a mistake, we wanted to be as cautious as we possibly could

After more than a month of praying and seeking counsel, almost all of the disadvantages disappeared! It became clear to us that this was the place that God had been preparing for us all along, so we put our little cabin up for sale.

After six months our cabin still had not sold, but, knowing that God was directing to progress, we moved out of our little cabin in faith in February of 2007, trusting that He would sell it in His timing. And He did! About six months later, we got a firm contract on the cabin. Not only that, we sold it for much more than double what we paid for it! That left us with money to put into favorite ministry projects, and also to help a very sick sister in the church.

God's timing was absolutely perfect! Our cabin sold in August of 2007—immediately prior to the real estate collapse in this area if the United States! God knew what He was doing! He is faithful!

We've now been living here in my mother's home for the past six years and it has been a wonderful blessing for all of us. Rachel was away at college by the time we moved in here, but she immensely enjoyed the beauty of the natural surroundings and having a larger kitchen to practice her culinary talents when she would come home.

We have been making some significant improvements to the home and property. The first thing we did, was to purchase (and have installed) a wood stove to provide our heating needs as we did not want the expense of central heat and air. The system was the wrong size to adequately heat a large home. We began expanding the garden the next year and made additional side plots to accommodate more crops. From year to year, we have added more plants; grape vines, a fig tree, and several more blueberry bushes. We added a comfrey patch for multi purpose use; herbal medicine, food and composting. We also added a perennial herb bed for culinary use.

The interesting thing about our sojourn in country living is that we did not always "see the big picture," everything that we needed to do, or how everything should fit together. But, God is faithful and he saw our "blind spots" and moved us along step by step as we went forward by faith and prayer.

The biggest challenge we have considered most recently is this: how do we become fully self-sustainable? We had our own ideas, but they were definitely faulty. But, God was so very faithful in making sure that our questions would be answered. Back in November, 2012 a mini-version of the Sustainable Preparedness Expo came to our area. Robin had to work that day and was unable to go, and I was not planning to go. But, providentially, God put certain people in my path to motivate me to go. This was where God gave us the vision to see "the bigger picture" of country living. By God's design, there was a booth there manned by SDA, Scott Esh, founder of Homestead Creations. I hadn't been going to many of the booths; I was mainly taking in the different lectures on various country living topics. But, near the end of the day I wandered back to Scott's booth, not really knowing why I had stopped there. He told me later that when I stopped it was one of the rare moments when he had five minutes to talk. By the time I came, he had been talking non-stop all day! I realized later that it was no fluke that I had stopped. It was the Holy Spirit that was prompting my movements that day. I spoke briefly with Scott, signed an "Interest Sheet" and he got in touch with us about a week later, explaining the work he did, which was helping folks know how to make everything work as it ought to work for a self-sustainable homestead. God had shown him over a period of many years how to "do" this and now he was helping others as a business/ministry to know how to navigate the challenges of "how" to do it, and do it right, without costly mistakes and/or spending too much money, etc.

Phase Four

We purchased Scott's services and are now in the next phase of country living—modifying our existing home in order to transition to an off-grid home with an integrated system that is designed to work and work right! Scott also helped us to see that we needed to further expand on the gardening space and further expand on the orchard trees (which has now already been partially accomplished). He helped us to see that we need to be in the best possible position to not only help ourselves but to also help, and be a blessing to, others. His services have been absolutely invaluable to us, and we are so incredibly delighted to see the hand of the Lord in having our paths intersect.

Though we have very little money to accomplish all that is still needed, we have seen that God has provided all that we required up to this point. Moving out in faith, we have every confidence that He will continue to provide our needs as we continue to covenant with Him in obedience to do our part. When we hardly knew how to pray for what we needed, God was already answering.

May you be encouraged to step out in faith also to begin the country sojourn! It is worth it all! We say again, that God is "…is a rewarder of them that diligently seek Him." (Heb. 11:6)

CHAPTER

NINETEEN

Still His Plan

DAVE WESTBROOK

Build ye houses, and dwell in them;
and plant gardens and eat the fruit of them
Jeremiah 29:5

Are you ready to find your place in the country? If you answered "Yes" to that question, and if you clicked on Dave Westbrook's "Country Living University" website then you're at the right place. At Country Living University you'll find everything you need to know to get your family out of the city and start pursuing your country living dream. Dave and Laura offer online training videos, webinars and more. They have not stumbled upon their knowledge by accident. The Lord, providentially, led them out of the city. Here is their story. Their message to the reader is, "The Lord will do the same for you! It's His plan!"

Our country living story began in 1997. Previous to that we lived in the desert town of Fallon, Nevada. It was a cute little house in town on a postage stamp lot with neighbors on every side. I was the pastor of the Seventh-day Adventist church there. We enjoyed our neighbors, but our hearts began to long for a place to live in the mountains. We longed for trees and meadows and desired to be surrounded by the beautiful scenes of nature. When the call came from the conference to consider relocating to a church district close to the mountains, we praised God. So it was, in 1997, that we accepted the call to pastor the Carson City Church and moved to the Nevada side of South Lake Tahoe.

Those were great years which bring back many fond memories. We moved into a townhouse with a view of Lake Tahoe and Mt. Tallac. It was there, in the Sierra Nevada Mountains, that many changes began taking place in my thinking as I began studying more and more earnestly in the Bible and the Spirit of Prophecy. It was during those years that I discovered powerful truths given to us in the writings of Ellen G. White. One of those truths had to do with the call to God's people to leave the cities.

Although we lived in the mountains, we soon discovered that South Lake Tahoe was simply a city in the mountains. Heavy traffic and neighbors on all sides once again caused us to consider whether or not God had something better in mind. It was during those years that we were blessed with the birth of our first child, Allison. As she grew, we knew that we needed a place for her to run free. We also needed room for a garden.

First Country Living Experience

In the summer of 2000, we had the opportunity to spend some time on a secluded piece of property in northern California. There was a small a-frame cabin with no phone lines and no cell phone service. Our only electricity came from a generator. There we started our country living training, learning to deal with mice, mosquitoes, and open range cows. By the end of that tough summer, we were praying earnestly for the Lord to guide us to just the right spot.

That was a difficult time. Here I was, the pastor who had been preaching to his city congregation that the time had come to leave, yet it seemed that we could not find our own country home. I remember telling the Lord, "If I've been wrong about this, show me. If we're really not supposed to leave the city yet, I'm willing to stay. Please help me understand from your Word." So I went back to study the subject again, only to find even more compelling evidence that it was indeed time to leave.

Meanwhile, Laura was making a list of requirements for our country property. She was inspired by Deuteronomy 6:10, 11:

And it shall be, when the LORD thy God shall have brought thee into the land which he sware unto thy fathers, to Abraham, to Isaac, and to Jacob, to give thee great and goodly cities, which thou buildedst not, And houses full of all good things, which thou filledst not, and wells digged, which thou diggedst not, vineyards and olive trees, which thou plantedst not; when thou shalt have eaten and be full.

I thought my wife wanted too much. Some of the items on her list included:

◆ Home on a meadow surrounded by trees

- ♦ Mountain views
- ♦ An orchard
- ♦ No mosquitoes

"Laura", I reasoned, "We're living in a world of sin. Someone has to have mosquitoes and it's probably us."

Serious Search Begins

During the next couple of months we looked earnestly, following leads with logging companies, driving for miles and spending countless hours scouting the country side. At times it was exasperating. One day

we noticed an ad in an old edition of the Pacific Union Recorder. It sounded ideal. The only thing we couldn't figure out was why we hadn't seen it before as we were periodically checking the Recorder for Real Estate ads. We called the phone number listed in the ad but it had been disconnected. I told Laura I was sure the place was sold as it seemed so ideal and was offered at such a reasonable price. But there was an e-mail address listed in the ad, so I sent them a quick note, asking if the property was still available. Days passed with no response.

Then one day, as I was driving back from a long trip in search of property which, once again, had proven fruitless, I had a heart to heart conversation with the Lord. Just then I was passing through a particularly lovely valley. I said, "Lord, there has to be a place for us around here somewhere!" Just at that moment, it seemed the Lord was very near. It was not an audible voice, but the names of church members came to mind, "So-and-so's place is here, and so-and-so's place is here – but your place is not here."

I immediately responded, "O.K. Lord, if our place is not here, where is it? I am willing to go! Why did you make me go through all of this looking if you have something in mind somewhere else?" Once again, the message was clear – "Because Dave, that's the only way you'd be convinced."

It was as if that was the Lord's way of telling me that he had something for us that was completely out of our geographic area. Even though I didn't get the exact answer as to what and where, I returned home with a peace that God was leading.

The very next day, I received an e-mail response regarding the property we had seen listed in the Recorder. It had been about two weeks since I had sent my inquiry. Indeed, the property had already sold, but the sender told me of another property just up the road which sounded interesting. So, I called the owner and as he described his property to me, it fit perfectly the description from Laura's list. After hanging up with the owner, I immediately called her and said,

"I think I just found our property."

"Really? Where is it?" she asked.

"It's in Washington State."

"Washington!" Neither of us were interested in moving that far away from family and friends, but we decided to go and see the property.

Reading Providences

It was an icy day in January of 2001 when we arrived at the property for the first time. The home was unfinished, with eight bedrooms, four baths, two kitchens, and two living rooms. There was an orchard with various kinds of fruit trees, as well as a hundred blueberry bushes. The property was half timber and half meadow with sweeping views of the surrounding mountains. It seemed to have everything on Laura's list. As the owner and I were walking alone, I suddenly remembered one more thing – mosquitoes! I was sure it had to have those! So I asked, "Do you have mosquitoes here?" The owner thought for a moment, and said – "I think I've seen one mosquito in 16 years."

As we made the trip home, we were elated. It seemed we'd found our place, but now how to pay for it? We believed that if God wanted us to purchase the property, He could provide a way. So we began contemplating our options. We had saved up some money, but of course it was not enough to buy a home outright. So I decided to study, in the Spirit of Prophecy, the issue of borrowing. My conclusion was that while we should avoid debt, there were times when borrowing was acceptable. The purchase of property could be one such case. (Note: I should add that we must be very careful about borrowing. If you feel you must borrow, it is much better if you can find a private lender rather than borrow funds from a bank. We are moving quickly into times in which it will be very advantageous not to be indebted to any financial institution.)

Late one Friday afternoon, our excitement about our new country home was interrupted by a phone call. "How far is the nearest fire hydrant?" asked the agent. "I have no idea," I responded, "this place is in the country." The agent asked, "Well, is there a hydrant within one-thousand feet?"

"One-thousand feet? Definitely not! I don't know of a fire hydrant for miles!" I informed the surprised agent.

"Well, that's going to be a problem. Our underwriter will not allow that." No insurance, no mortgage – the deal would be off!

Praying It Through

What could we do but pray? Even though it seemed that we could see the Lord's hand each step of the way, we told Him we were willing to give it up if that was His will. But we pled with the Lord, "If this is the place you want us to have, please open this door." As we researched, we soon found that many insurance companies will not insure rural properties. But it turned out that there was a local Grange that offered insurance even without fire hydrants, and at very reasonable rates.

Meanwhile, a remarkable thing had happened. We had received a notice in the mail that our rent at Lake Tahoe was going up from $800 to $1,000 per month! We had faithfully paid our rent so I drove down to the property management and asked what the problem was. They informed me that the owner had discovered that she could have been making a lot more money, and wanted the rent raised to $1,200, but they had convinced her not to do that just yet, for fear of losing the current renters. That seemed like just one more sign that we were supposed to move.

The Lord blessed, and we were moved out of the townhouse before the rent went up, and found ourselves driving north with the biggest U-Haul truck available. We moved into our country home on March 1, 2001. I wish I could say that it was just a bed of roses after that, but that is not the case. We confronted many challenges. The house was unfinished and I had to learn some basic building skills. I also had to learn to do simple household repairs, since the repairman could be as much as an hour away. Then, the snow melted, revealing piles of junk on the property that we had to clean up. There were the stresses of the unknown, as we waited upon the Lord, not sure how everything would work out.

One of the questions we faced was how we would make a living after moving to a very rural setting. I had prayed fervently that the Lord would guide me so that I would not take my family into difficulty unnecessarily. I asked Him to show me if I was being presumptuous. If so, I was willing to scrap the whole thing. During the first two and one-half years after moving, I continued to work part time for the Nevada-

Utah Conference. We had also launched a little faith ministry called "Back to Enoch," and so I was accepting invitations to travel and speak in various places. It was amazing to see how the Lord provided for our needs. I was working only quarter time for the conference, so that meant our regular paycheck was cut by seventy-five percent. But God was faithful, and we never had a time when we couldn't pay our bills.

Country Characters

It has been through obstacles and difficulties that the Lord has worked on our characters. There are those who refer to the difficulties of country living as an argument against making the move out of the city. They will sometimes point to the experience of someone who became discouraged by the challenges and gave up — moving back to the city — as an argument in favor of staying in the city. I have come to believe that the obstacles and difficulties of country living are, in themselves, one of the most important reasons why God calls us to make this change. Notice the following quote from the writings of Ellen White:

So with the great majority of the best and noblest men of all ages. Read the history of Abraham, Jacob, and Joseph; of Moses, David, and Elisha. Study the lives of men of later times who have most worthily filled positions of trust and responsibility.

"How many of these were reared in country homes. They knew little of luxury. They did not spend their youth in amusement. Many were forced to struggle with poverty and hardship. They early learned to work, and their active life in the open air gave vigor and elasticity to all their faculties. Forced to depend upon their own resources, they learned to combat difficulties and to surmount obstacles, and they gained courage and perseverance. They learned the lessons of self-reliance and self-control. Sheltered in a great

degree from evil associations, they were satisfied with natural pleasures and wholesome companionships. They were simple in their tastes and temperate in their habits. They were governed by principle, and they grew up pure and strong and true. When called to their lifework, they brought to it physical and mental power, buoyancy of spirit, ability to plan and execute, and steadfastness in resisting evil that made them a positive power for good in the world (*The Adventist Home*, p. 134).

Miracles, Blessings, Promises

Through the years since we moved to the country, we've seen many miracles and felt blessed to be surrounded by nature with beautiful sunsets, fruit trees, berries, produce from our garden, and wonderful visits with those who have come to our home in the mountains. So many times after a trip to town, or upon returning from a speaking appointment, I find myself thanking God as I come up our driveway and through the meadow to our quiet country home. Indeed, I have felt that we live like "kings and queens":

"But the earth has blessings hidden in her depths for those who have courage and will and perseverance to gather her treasures. Fathers and mothers who possess a piece of land and a comfortable home are kings and queens" (*Fundamentals of Christian Education*, pp. 326, 327).

In God's plan for Israel every family had a home on the land, with sufficient ground for tilling. Thus were provided both the means and the incentive for a useful, industrious, and self-supporting life. And no devising of men has ever improved upon that plan (*Counsels to Parents, Teachers, and Students*, p. 275).

Did you notice in the above statement Mrs. White said that that was the plan for "every family" in Israel? Could it be that it is *still* God's plan? I believe it is, and the purpose of this book is to help you find that "piece of land and a comfortable home" that God has in mind for you. Remember, it's His promise to you:

God will help His people to find such homes outside of the cities (*The Adventist Home*, p. 13).

Go to David Westbrook's web site, http://countrylivinguniversity.com, to learn about his outreach ministry, *Country Living University* designed specifically to help those who want to learn more about how to make a successful move to the country.

TWENTY

Together, To Heaven

LINDA FRANKLIN

Get ready, get ready, get ready. Ye must have a greater preparation than ye now have… Sacrifice all to God. Lay all upon His altar self, property, and all, a living sacrifice. It will take all to enter glory. Lay up for yourselves treasure in heaven, where no thief can approach or rust corrupt. Ye must be partakers of Christ's sufferings here if ye would be partakers with Him of His glory hereafter. Heaven will be cheap enough, if we obtain it through suffering. We must deny self all along the way, die to self daily, let Jesus alone appear, and keep His glory continually in view (Early Writings, 66).

Is there any pastime more rewarding and encouraging than to read the glimpses of heaven recorded in the Bible and then try, with a sanctified imagination, to view our real homeland? Everything we experience here on earth is a preparation for eternal glories, if we so choose. Until we get to heaven, God will lead us on the pathway out of the world and toward heaven. Is there a more apt description of the sacrifices and rewards on our homeward journey than The Impressive Dream?

I dreamed of being with a large body of people. A portion of this assembly started out prepared to journey. We had heavily loaded wagons. As we journeyed, the road seemed to ascend. On one side of this road was a deep precipice; on the other was a high, smooth, white wall, like the hard finish upon plastered rooms. As we journeyed on, the road grew narrower and steeper. In some places it seemed so very narrow that we concluded that we could no longer travel with the loaded wagons. We then loosed them from the horses, took a portion of the luggage from the wagons and placed it upon the horses, and journeyed on horseback.

As we progressed, the path still continued to grow narrow. We were obliged to press close to the wall, to save ourselves from falling off the narrow road down the steep precipice. As we did this, the luggage on the horses pressed against the wall and caused us to sway toward the precipice. We feared that we should fall and be dashed in pieces on the rocks. We then cut the luggage from the horses, and it fell over the precipice. We continued on horseback, greatly fearing, as we came to the narrower places in the road, that we should lose our balance and fall. At such times a hand seemed to take the bridle and guide us over the perilous way.

As the path grew more narrow, we decided that we could no

longer go with safety on horseback, and we left the horses and went on foot, in single file, one following in the footsteps of another. At this point small cords were let down from the top of the pure white wall; these we eagerly grasped, to aid us in keeping our balance upon the path. As we traveled, the cord moved along with us. The path finally became so narrow that we concluded that we could travel more safely without our shoes, so we slipped them from our feet and went on some distance without them. Soon it was decided that we could travel more safely without our stockings; these were removed, and we journeyed on with bare feet.

We then thought of those who had not accustomed themselves to privations and hardships. Where were such now? They were not in the company. At every change some were left behind, and those only remained who had accustomed themselves to endure hardships. The privations of the way only made these more eager to press on to the end.

Our danger of falling from the pathway increased. We pressed close to the white wall, yet could not place our feet fully upon the path, for it was too narrow. We then suspended nearly our whole weight upon the cords, exclaiming: "We have hold from above! We have hold from above!" The same words were uttered by all the company in the narrow pathway. As we heard the sounds of mirth and revelry that seemed to come from the abyss below, we shuddered. We heard the profane oath, the vulgar jest, and low, vile songs. We heard the war song and the dance song. We heard instrumental music and loud laughter, mingled with cursing and cries of anguish and bitter wailing, and were more anxious than ever to keep upon the narrow, difficult pathway. Much of the time we were compelled to suspend our whole weight upon the cords, which increased in size as we progressed.

I noticed that the beautiful white wall was stained with blood. It caused a feeling of regret to see the wall thus stained. This feeling, however, lasted but for a moment, as I soon thought that it was all as it should be. Those who are following after will know that others have passed the narrow, difficult way before them, and will conclude that if others were able to pursue their onward course, they can do the same. And as the blood shall be pressed from their aching feet, they will not faint with discouragement; but, seeing the blood upon the wall, they will know that others have endured the same pain.

At length we came to a large chasm, at which our path ended. There was nothing now to guide the feet, nothing upon which to rest them. Our whole reliance must be upon the cords, which had increased in size until they were as large as our bodies. Here we were for a time thrown into perplexity and distress. We inquired in fearful whispers: "To what is the cord attached?" My husband was just before me. Large drops of sweat were falling from his brow, the veins in his neck and temples were increased to double their usual size, and suppressed, agonizing groans came from his lips. The sweat was dropping from my face, and I felt such anguish as I had never felt before. A fearful struggle was before us. Should we fail here, all the difficulties of our journey had been experienced for nought.

Before us, on the other side of the chasm, was a beautiful field

*of green grass, about six inches high. I could not see the sun;
but bright, soft beams of light, resembling fine gold and silver,
were resting upon this field. Nothing I had seen upon earth
could compare in beauty and glory with this field. But could
we succeed in reaching it? was the anxious inquiry. Should the
cord break, we must perish. Again, in whispered anguish, the
words were breathed: "What holds the cord?" For a moment
we hesitated to venture. Then we exclaimed: "Our only hope is
to trust wholly to the cord. It has been our dependence all the
difficult way. It will not fail us now." Still we were hesitating
and distressed. The words were then spoken: "God holds the
cord. We need not fear." These words were then repeated by
those behind us, accompanied with: "He will not fail us now.
He has brought us thus far in safety."*

*My husband then swung himself over the fearful abyss into the
beautiful field beyond. I immediately followed. And, oh, what
a sense of relief and gratitude to God we felt! I heard voices
raised in triumphant praise to God. I was happy, perfectly
happy.*

*I awoke, and found that from the anxiety I had experienced in
passing over the difficult route, every nerve in my body seemed
to be in a tremor. This dream needs no comment. It made such
an impression upon my mind that probably every item in it
will be vivid before me while my memory shall continue (Testimonies for the Church, vol. 2, p. 596-597).*

The prophet Isaiah shares a verse that gives us a "hands-on" glimpse of
how our boundless energies will be employed—building and planting;

And they shall build houses, and inhabit [them]; and they shall plant vineyards, and eat the fruit of them (Isaiah 65:21).

Some folks will be out of a job; there will be no need for doctors and nurses, politicians, firemen, policemen, lighting technicians, and laundry services to name a few. But, until then, we have a work to do in our character, in order to become Christ like. In His mercy, He is putting us with folks that reveal the weaknesses we must overcome, not by behavioral modification but by total surrender. He will take me from my 25th floor downtown apartment, to a home in the country that He has prepared with just the right amount of trials calculated to manifest what is in my heart. How else could I learn to know myself, except He asks me to get along with my neighbor?

I can't imagine a more sanctified method of Him preparing us for heaven in these end times, than allowing us to become part of a survival team. The remnant of a bolt of cloth usually has a few wrinkles and imperfections, but it hangs together until the very end. The remnant is just what is needed to finish the integrated tapestry of His love. It is a picture knit together in love.

Unity and Talents

God is serious about unity. Christ's final prayer in the Garden of Gethsemane (John 17:11, 22) is that His people may be one; one with Him so that they may be one with each other. This end-time-advice (about moving away from the cities) that appears throughout the Spirit of Prophecy with sincere urgency, will require a unity that most of us have not yet experienced.

After presenting the urgency of this message, we often see desperation in the eyes of the elderly, the infirm, the single parents, the widows. They ask, "How can I do what you say I should do; I have no money, I have no strength, I have no skill, etc." Lay your fears right there beside your desires on the altar and turn again to the promise: *God will help His people find such homes outside the cities.*

Practical Group Dynamics

Learning to get along with others is the practical application of Christianity: love to God, love to our fellow man, and the golden rule just about takes care of the tendency toward self-indulgence. In the end times Jesus reveals that the one distinction of His people will be that we love each other (John 13:35). We will have finally learned the meaning of preferring one another (Romans 12:20). We have difficulty when we fail to be sensitive to the needs of others, usually by our ignorance of their need. Interestingly, the sin of ignorance also cost the life of a lamb, or other animal, under the old dispensation. Since we cannot afford to cause harm, here is a list of sensitive areas and simple suggestions that will help us avoid causing offence as we learn to work together in a home or group setting:

Leadership:

1) Direction; agreement on interpretation of scripture and the Spirit of Prophecy.

2) Spiritual Education: conduct classes on topics pertinent to salvation and group dynamics (i.e. The Beautiful Way, Coming Events, True Education, Privilege of Worship, etc. Group study can also include folks from other communities,

3) Vision: keep members working as a team.

4) Discipline: teach principles of self-governance and respect.

Family Values: Follow a schedule: worship (individual and group), practice the concept of children staying with parents, have a time for work, study, and recreational time (non-competitive).

Agriculture: one farmer leads (under God) requesting group energies one-half day. (Agricultural needs have priority summer and winter!) Household Maintenance: water, sanitation (scheduled washing of clothes, toilet, microbiological issues, etc.), building and repairs, etc.

Culture Groups: Where there is more than one family on a country property, we recommend same culture groups where possible, as there are certain environmental concepts that are comfortable to one culture that might be offensive to another. If this is not possible, then work together toward a goal-oriented unity of spirit.

Dress: durable, modest clothing, reflecting the distinctness between men and women, and the purity that becomes a Christian.

Diet:

  1) respect for one cook (under God) with helpers as needed,

  2) simple food prepared in a wholesome way,

  3) spiritually dedicated appetite (ongoing group education).

  4) the principle of survival is sharing.

Golden Rule: By either word or act, do nothing offensive; treat others as you want to be treated. Your marriage, even today, can be strengthened be enacting this principle; is there anything you are doing alone (or together) that is offending a pure and Holy God?

Problem solving: Do not attempt to solve a problem after 9 PM, or at mealtimes (keep meals cheerful), or during an emotional outburst (this may intensify reactivity).

Sensitivity: concern for others is good, concern for self is not!

Sensitivity

It is our conclusion after answering countless questions from many audiences that the end times will require a level of unity and skilful sensitivity to each other's needs that is currently unknown among good-hearted Christians. Group dynamics will be at an entirely different level of people skills; far beyond simple behavior modification in order to control tempers, sharp tongues, and accusatory remarks. Success in these last days will require total character renewal according to God's law, especially His Golden Rule. Gone will be the inferences and spin-offs of the early disciples' strife over "Who is the Greatest?" Our spiritual leaders at that time will be the humblest, most practical, self-sacrificing of servants. They will be simple, quiet folk who have become sensitive to the voice of God as they went about their daily work.

Unexpected talent will be developed in those in the common walks of life. If men and women can only have the message of truth brought to them, many who hear will receive it. Those of every rank of life, high and low, rich and poor, will accept the truth for this time. Some who are regarded as uneducated will be called to the service of the Master, even as the humble, unlearned fishermen were called by the Saviour. Men will be called from the plow, as was Elisha, and will be moved to take up the work that God has appointed them. They will begin to labor in simplicity and quietness, reading and explaining the Scriptures to others. Their simple efforts will be successful (*This Day With God*, p.115).

A generation of dear saints who endured the Great Depression by subsistence farming will blend sensationally with the "Text Generation" who probably haven't given much thought to the food they buy with a swipe of their convenience card. The old times will be return; gone are all those little plastic cards. Our paycheck will be a head of cabbage, a jar of garden stew, a handful of dried berries to share with the family of God. It may well be that only those who have seed to plant and a place to plant it will be among those alive at Christ's return. Recent evidence reveals that our diet can be greatly simplified and still satisfy our nutritional needs. We may finally have to surrender our preferences to principle; for instance, we have searched, unsuccessfully through our seed catalogues for doughnut seeds and sandwich cookie bulbs!

God's final remnant is characterized by a group of people with a sense of unity so strong that they will be able to communicate His love to each other in ways heretofore unparalleled. This unity is to begin now and strengthen with the passage of time until it cannot be broken. It is a soul saving dynamic that calls for a closeness, a stronger Holy Spirit affinity, than any group of humans has yet experienced. It is more tender than any earthly ties we will ever know; it is above any inducement or bribe, more final than death; it never stoops to offend or take offence; it is even stronger than our own opinion!

As long as we hold to our own ideas and opinions with determined persistency, we cannot have the unity for which Christ prayed (*Testimonies to Ministers*, p. 30).

Before the final visitation of God's judgments upon the earth there will be among the people of the Lord such a revival of primitive godliness as has not been witnessed since apostolic times. The Spirit and power of God will be poured out upon His children (*The Great Controversy*, p. 464).

This group that is lead by the Spirit will form stronger than earthly ties in order to accomplish His deep designs as the earth begins its final heavings. They will, as in the days of Pentecost, be inspired by love to truly care for the needs of each other. Acts 4 tells of a time when the disciples, possessed by the Holy Spirit, had all things common. Isaiah speaks of a time when; *They helped every one his neighbour; and [every one] said to his brother, Be of good courage* (Isaiah 41:6). Though it is also a mark of discipleship today, members of God's true remnant will never indulge in a comfort that causes pain to another person.

Although it would do well for us to practice Christ likeness today, characteristics of the remnant at the end of time will include those who are: humble, teachable, energetic, pure-minded, holy, unselfish, quiet, kind, lovers of truth and righteousness. They will form unlikely, yet symbiotic relationships; an energetic young man who is ignorant about the dynamics of agriculture adopts a grandfather who knows how to grind a fine edge on a hoe and loves the dirt; a retired couple purchases a farm (agricultural land, water available at a hand pump, wood for heating and building, and good air) and teams up with a displaced farmer whose family knows and loves the soil and has the energy it takes to follow the crop from planting till harvest; a young lady who has neither sewn nor sown finds a great-grandmother who can, and cans, too! No one man (or woman) will have all of the answers, but with a willingness to make God's love and law number one, and prayer with sisters and brothers in the family of God number two, we can not only survive, we can thrive in spite of our circumstances. What does Isaiah 58 say about our health springing forth speedily as a result of being sensitive to the needs of others?

Advice from Uncle David

I recently heard an inspiring sermon by David Gates, leader of *Gospel Ministry*, a well-established worldwide missionary outreach program. His volunteers are from assorted backgrounds and personalities, with human strengths and weaknesses. In his sermon he mentioned that he had been asked this question: "Pastor David, How do you find all these perfect people who join you in mission work?" His response was something about there being no perfect people (yet) and that we must learn to appreciate the qualities that God can use in each of us. In a recent e-mail, I asked Brother Gates how we can minimize humanity and maximize sainthood. Here is Pastor David's answer for successful teamwork.

The Bible teaches that we can expect a real explosion of mission activity during the Loud Cry, so God will have to solve the human issues through the Holy Spirit.

On the practical side, if a person is truly converted and humble, almost any problem can be fixed with some good administration and balanced decisions. When the attitude is not good, I have never seen a good fix. Some people have emotional baggage that makes it very difficult to find a place for them to work even if they are converted and love the Lord. For these people we try our best to find something that they can live with. Sometimes it works and sometimes not.

The other great challenge is to match personalities. Two aggressive personalities will clash, so some space must be kept between some of your best people. They are generally highly productive—make big mistakes sometimes—but get things done. They are very valuable and need to be cared for and protected, as well as your other staff protected from getting run over by them! Divine wisdom is what God gives us to make decisions.

I could go on, but will mention one more thing. There has to be a clear line of authority established. When there are issues that can't be resolved, someone eventually has to have the authority to make the final decision which is accepted by all parties. Authority is not to micromanage anyone, but in helping to resolve issues that do not solve themselves and to set general vision and direction. Authority is greatest when combined with respect—respect that is earned, usually through caring and service of others.

A Call To Wholeness

With the outpouring of the Holy Spirit we can expect healing—and the most important aspect of healing is the healed heart. *The renewing of the heart is a far greater miracle than the healing of the diseases of the body* (Manuscript Releases, vol. 9, p. 281)

By taking the cross of Christ, we are called to the ministry of reconciliation, in keeping with 2 Corinthians 5:18; *And all things [are] of God, who hath reconciled us to himself by Jesus Christ, and hath given to us the ministry of reconciliation.*

How would a person know that they needed healing? It's a matter of being able to get along with people; if you feel other folks have to change before you can associate with them, then you are in need. If you are angry, emotionally explosive, then your frayed feelings, like frazzled wires, need repair. If you cannot show affection, look for God to lean down and ask, "Wilt Thou be made whole?" and then accept His touch upon your broken places. He will show you the wound from which you need to heal. If you allow folks to step on you without expressing your displeasure, then you need to learn and set your boundaries, which is another form of healing. Everyone who survives the end times will experience a level of emotional healing that will allow them to be useful in God's Kingdom of peace. Knowing our true value in God's eyes, we will not be crippled by false humility nor pridefully self-sufficient. He will be able to use us to reach others for the Kingdom. Seeds that remain unplanted cannot bear fruit, and soil that remains uncultivated cannot nurture the seeds of truth.

Validation, Justification, Responsibility

There is one very simple concept of peace-keeping that everyone can apply. If someone is offended, consider them the expert on their feelings; that is; *validate* the possibility that you have hurt them, assume the blame, and ask forgiveness. This de-fuses the sparking mechanism. If someone has hurt you, you have the right to go to that person (regardless of how far in the past your pain occurred) and say, "What you said (or did) hurt me deeply." This is where the rubber of forgiveness meets the pavement of heaven's highway; gracefully accepting responsibility.

The art of getting along with people has diminished with city living. Although the Dirty Thirties contained many ugly aspects, families stayed together for survival. There is no need to re-invent the wheel when it comes to getting along with each other. With the true unity of the end times, self will take the beating it justly deserves. Opinions will be laid aside. Non-salvational issues will be given low priority since they introduce controversial topics to no purpose. Sentimental trinkets are discarded. Our stuff will be will be in as compact a compass as possible, and whatever we have is subject to His request to share. If I have two coats, I will give the second one to someone with a greater need.

When we in any way justify our reason for hurting someone, we greatly diminish the possibility of our apology accomplishing any good, but by accepting responsibility, spiritual growth is accomplished. This mechanism applies to any age group, in any walk of life. Even in non-Christian counseling practices, the attitude of total forgiveness is the ultimate goal. Forgiveness is the gift we give ourselves. It's a great stress reducer! Try it—it is one of the ways that we can taste and see that the Lord is good.

Many "grown-up children" carry father-or mother-wounds with them to the grave. Unresolved pain not only hurts the one who carries it, it hurts those around this person. Their influence for good is crippled. Wounded people either over-react or are under-attached. Instead of helping others discover the joy of God's love, the breach widens. We are here solely to demonstrate God's love or Satan's sentimental deceptions. Old wounds require the salve of lies. Satan will do anything within his power to keep us from discovering the joy of surrendering our wounds to The Great Physician and discovering the joy of walking in truth.

God has bound our hearts to Him by unnumbered tokens in heaven and in earth. Through the things of nature, and the deepest and tenderest earthly ties that human hearts can know, He has sought to reveal Himself to us (*Steps to Christ*, p. 10).

There are ways to apply balm and heal the wounded heart of a grownup child, even one who has existed in a world of deception so long that he or she is no longer able to discern truth from error. The Great Physician is still asking, "Wilt thou be made whole?" The wound, to heal, must be carefully lanced, following the admission of the wound that cannot be healed without the touch of the Great Physician. Write about the wound; this gets it out of the infected heart where one can read the description and place it on the altar, and from there, be dealt with in an attitude of forgiveness. Freedom to live truth is a priceless treasure.

Skeletons

How do we clean out the skeletons in our closet that haunt us with accusatory voices from the past? One of the most effective ways for most people is to write down specific events and definite feelings (anger, jealousy, rejection, etc.), and then take time to process the hurtful memories. Ask God's forgiveness for carrying the burden so long. The healing comes as we become willing to see the damage we have caused, to our own life and the lives of others. Most people experience freedom by releasing the damaging secret they have held by telling the person who hurt them: 1) how they hurt you, 2) how your life was damaged, 3) that you forgive them (even if they see no reason to be forgiven).

There is a wonderful Bible promise that applies to the end times; it's as if our families will be in unity, or our land will not produce.

Behold, I will send you Elijah the prophet before the coming of the great and dreadful day of the LORD; And *he shall turn the heart of the fathers to the children, and the heart of the children to their fathers, lest I come and smite the earth with a curse.* (Malachi 4:5,6).

Forgiving others is the only way to find our own forgiveness. By accepting His invitation to forgive, we realize the gift ourselves. There is no other way.

Strong Character Needed

How will the Lord prepare His people? By allowing trials to reveal the condition of the heart. An unchristlike reaction to provocation means that the place of full surrender has not yet been discovered. A true Christian will never be found aggravating another person, including their children (Ephesians 6:4).One who relies on behavioral modification, however pleasant the person may appear, will not wrestle successfully through Jacob's Time of Trouble. Jacob was a deceiver, but he gained the blessing he sought, and, was able to win back his brother by persevering in prayer. Peace-making is a blessing from the Lord in answer to the prayer of faith. We shall have to not only survive the severe living conditions ahead of us, we shall have to do whatever is asked with a sweet spirit!

The season of distress and anguish before us will require a faith that can endure weariness, delay, and hunger—a faith that will not faint though severely tried. The period of probation is granted to all to prepare for that time. Jacob prevailed because he was persevering and determined. His victory is an evidence of the power of importunate prayer. All who will lay hold of God's promises, as he did, and be as earnest and persevering as he was, will succeed as he succeeded. Those who are unwilling to deny self, to agonize before God, to pray long and earnestly for His blessing, will not obtain it (*The Great Controversy*, p. 621).

Too Late, or Right On Time?

As the Holy Spirit is withdrawn from the earth, those who dedicate themselves to God's will, moment by moment, will discern His voice and follow His direction, step by step. Too late, some will ask, "Is there any word from the Lord?" (Jeremiah 37:17). Heart-changes cannot be postponed for a more convenient season. When He says it's time for change, to accept healing, a willing heart will answer.

The man at the pool of Bethesda had waited a long time for healing. Yet, Christ asked the man before He touched him, if he truly desired healing. A person who accepts Jesus' healing touch must place himself in a vulnerable position. He must admit that He is helpless to change himself. He must surrender His broken places. He must accept the invitation to never return to what he once was. No addiction can withstand the healing touch of the Saviour. Heaven begins with this healing touch.

Heaven begins now. By rightly valuing every soul, we can begin today to envision heaven and help each other toward that bright land. I ask myself, "Is the desire for that heavenly country in my heart?" If it is, I will be intent on sharing, for that is the purpose of the journey heavenward.

God's Plan of Escape
From the city, to a home in the country,
to the wilderness, and finally to heaven.

Frequently Asked Questions at YCS Seminars

As we present our weekend seminars about being ready for end time events, we conclude some of our meetings with a question and answer period. The following are some of the most frequently asked questions accompanied by our answers.

1. **Q: If God will protect us anyway, why should we move out of the cities?**

   A: The most obvious answer would be that He *asked* us to move out. First, it is the safest place to raise children and address the needs of our own character development in preparing for heaven. Second, it will be in the cities that the judgments and plagues will fall. Those who follow His counsel, as in the days of the destruction of Jerusalem, will not be found in the city. Our only protection is in listening to His counsel and following His plan (Psalm 91:9, 10).

2. **Q: Where is country? Is it a certain distance from the city? How will I know when I am in the country?**

   A: Country is not necessarily a place, or a certain distance from town; it's what you can do there. If you have good agricultural land on which to grow your food, are allowed to have an outhouse, can pump water by hand, have a large buffer zone of acreage to insure elbow room where you can see no other houses, and have fuel in the form of wood so that you can cook and heat your home, then you are, most likely, in the place we call "country".

3.   **Q: How will we pay our taxes during the time of no buy-no sell?**

A: I suggest prepaying your taxes. Many counties allow a large deposit on which they will pay you interest on the balance.

4.   **Q: How is it that I have been an Adventist my whole life and never understood that this "out of the cities" message is applicable today?**

A: God has given us the Bible and the Spirit of Prophecy for advice for these last days and the events just ahead of us. It is time that we rediscover these counsels for ourselves and to understand the messages that they contain. You may want to read my earlier book that deals with preparing for the time of no buy-no sell, *You Can Survive!* (available from your local ABC store, or Ruth Maddy: 1-509-369-2671).

5.   **Q: What if I am in debt**

A: Jesus says that we should shun debt like the leprosy (*Testimonies for the Church*, vol. 6, page 217). With the command is the promise for success (*Education*, page 126). When the time of no buy-no sell comes (Revelation 13:17) we will not be able to pay debts. Now is the time to be debt-free. If we are not debt-free, then we are in a trap which the world will hold over our heads and enslave us when we are unable to pay. (See also chapter 9 in *You Can Survive!* on financial preparations.)

6.   **Q: How will we find work in the country?**

A: Our experience is that God will supply all of our needs (Philippians 4:19). When we came to British Columbia, we found work when we had less than a hundred dollars in our pocket! Later, we developed our own greenhouse business, and have been self employed for over twenty years. Discover a home-based business or "cottage industry" that you enjoy. Many folks are working from their homes, now.

7. **Q: We don't have any money, how will we pay for property?**

   A: *Medical Ministry*, page 310 tells us, *God will help His people find such homes outside the cities.* Acquaint yourself with stories of people who were able to find country property with no money, no job, and were even in debt!

8. **Q: If we are out in the country how will we do evangelism?**

   A: *Evangelism*, page 77: *We are to work the cities from outposts.* Once we have located in the country we do not hermitize, but seek to witness to others about God's plan for evangelism and about the soon return of Jesus. *God does not mean that any of us should become hermits or monks and retire from the world in order to devote ourselves to acts of worship. The life must be like Christ's life—between the mountain and the multitude (Steps to Christ,* page 101).

9. **Q: The church in the city will lose members if we all move out! How will it be supported?**

   A: *We are to be wise as serpents and harmless as doves in our efforts to secure country properties at a low figure, and from these outpost* *centers we are to work the cities. …We should plan our work in such a way as to keep our young people as far as possible from this contamination. The cities are to be worked from outposts. Said the messenger of God, "Shall not the cities be warned? Yes, not by God's people living in them, but by their visiting them, to warn them of what is coming upon the earth. As God's commandment-keeping people, we must leave the cities. As did Enoch, we must work in the cities but not dwell in them* (*Evangelism*, page 77). Again, the plan is for church members to establish outposts to train others in country living, still attending and financially supporting churches located in the city for purposes of evangelism.

10. Q: What are the characteristics of good country property?

A: We must have **wood** that will supply our needs for heat and for cooking for several years. We must have **land** on which we can raise our own provisions even if we can't go to the store. We must have **water** at the surface in form of a hand pump in a well *or* a spring on the hillside that will supply gravity pressure to our homes. These are three vital, basic components of the kind of property we need in anticipation of the time of no buy-no sell. (See *Country Living*, pages 9-10).

11. Q: Should our schools be in the country, too?

A: Yes. Please consider the following references: *If our schools are located in the cities it will be tenfold harder to develop spiritually for both parents and children* (*Fundamentals of Christian Education*, page 326). *All schools should be located in the country* (*Fundamentals of Christian Education*, page 322). And finally, *Never can the proper education be given unless our schools are located a wide distance from the cities* (*Life Sketches*, page 351).

12. Q: Should we hoard food?

A: Hoarding versus sharing—the first principle of survival is sharing. There will be no hoarding of food or other provisions during the time of trouble which occurs after the close of probation; *I saw that if the saints had food laid up by them or in the field in the time of trouble, when sword, famine, and pestilence are in the land, it would be taken from them by violent hands and strangers would reap their fields. Then will be the time for us to trust wholly in God and He will sustain us. I saw that our bread and water will be sure at that time and that we shall not lack or suffer hunger; for God is able to spread a table before us in the wilderness* (*Early Writings*, page 56). The principle of sharing was a miraculous phenomenon among survivors of Nazi concentration camps. Those who shared whatever scraps of food they found were more often among the survivors. Those who did not share, seemed less likely to survive. Sharing is our principle of operation, during the time ahead, to help everyone get to the kingdom. We can do this by sharing our essentials; food, water, wood, and shelter. We have been instructed to raise our own provisions. Because of His counsel, we dry, sprout, can, or store food in our root cellar to help us through the year until the next garden is harvestable.

13. Q: What about those things we can't provide for in the time of trouble, such as clothing?

A: Claim promises. An example comes from the experiences of the children of Israel during their wilderness wanderings for forty years. Their clothing did not wear out, neither did their shoes. Deuteronomy 29:5: *And I have led you 40 years in the wilderness: your clothes are not waxen old upon you, and thy shoe is not waxen old upon thy foot.* So it is for us; we will claim promises and ask

God to help us for the things the devil will bring upon us and those things which we cannot supply by the labor of our hands and the education of our hearts. In fact, the dedication of our hearts will make possible all that we need.

14. Q: Will there be some of us left behind as we flee?

A: No one gets left behind! Not unless they choose not to go on with us. As with Noah in the ark, when the door was shut there were those left behind who had chosen not to come into the ark. During the times ahead, we will leave no one behind who wishes to go with us, regardless of their physical health. God will provide for us in the most extenuating circumstances. *Yes, tell it in words full of cheer, that no one who perseveringly climbs the ladder will fail of gaining an entrance into the heavenly city* (*Messages to Young People*, page 95).

15. Q: How much attention should we give to conspiracy theories?

A: *The Great Controversy*, page 528 states that God's people know little of the devil's plots and that God will overrule everything that the devil thrusts upon us for the furtherance of His own deep designs. So, we will leave God to do His work, both at the head of the church (*Selected Messages, Book Two*, page 390) and in the world, though conspiracy theories appear to demand our immediate response. We do not have to respond to any conspiracy because they come in waves, and pass away just as quickly as the ocean tide.

16. Q: How will we travel during the time of no buy-no sell?

A: Travel restrictions will not hamper the Lord in getting His work accomplished. Philip was transported by the Spirit after presenting the gospel to the Ethiopian Prince, to (Acts 8:26-40). The Lord will transport us all at His second coming. If needed, He can transport us to witness in a certain place before He comes. If, today, we practice doing His bidding in the little things, then tomorrow He may be able use us to accomplish greater things in His name.

17. Q: How important is it to give our tithe to the church?

A: Originally the tithe was given to the Levites and placed in a storehouse outside the temple. Today, there are several voices telling us that we should pay tithe to the treasury of the remnant church. This means that the anti-type today is to provide support for ordained ministers and not be given to those called to a self-supporting ministry. I am not the treasury! (For a more complete study, see our brochure entitled *Tithe,* pages 6-10 which can be ordered from Ruth Maddy: ruth@youcansurvive.org, or 509-369-2671).

18. Q: We have noticed in your Power Point program that the ladies at Sanctuary Ranch who are involved in your ministry, wear dresses at all times. Why is that?

A: The ribbon of blue, mentioned in Numbers 15, and the statement about distinction of dress between men and women in Deuteronomy 22:5, both indicate that early in the experience of God's remnant people, dress was important. We are told that the ribbon of blue which was given to ancient Israel, is symbolized today by dress reform in God's remnant church (*Testimonies for the Church*, vol. 3, page 171). There are health reasons for dress reform as found in *Selected Messages*, Book Two, page 470. There is the element of female beauty of dress that lets people know of a commitment to God. (For more on this particular subject, refer to our brochure entitled *Ribbon of Blue* available from Ruth Maddy; ruth@youcansurvive.org, or 509-369-2671).

19 Q: What about Matthew 6:25, 31, and 34 where it says that we should not worry about provisions for tomorrow?
A: The text you refer to, *...take no thought for your life or what you shall eat...,* is counsel from Jesus for two different periods of time for daily need of food, clothing, and shelter, for today as well as the time after the close of probation when we make no preparations for our temporal wants (during the time of trouble: *Early Writings*, page 56).

Phil 4:19 says; *My God shall supply all your needs according to His riches in glory by Christ Jesus.* Matthew 6:34 pertains to our temporal wants as we live our daily life for it even says *Sufficient unto* **the day** *is the evil thereof.* (See Matthew 6:34: *Gospel Workers*, page 244, *Ministry of Healing*, page 481, and *Steps to Christ*, pages 121, 122).

Country Living, pages 9-10 states; *Again and again the Lord has instructed that our people are to take their families away from the cities, into the country, where they can raise their own provisions; for in the future the problem of buying and selling will be a very serious one.* I think you will see that the application of the verses in Matthew 6, when applied to preparation for the future, does not fit harmoniously with the voluminous counsel to move out of the cities and prepare for the Lord's second coming. Both counsels are authored by the same Lord.

20 **Q: Our schools—what will we do to have them ready for our Lord's return?**

A: *Before we can carry the message of present truth in all its fullness to other countries, we must first break every yoke. We must come into line of true education, walking in the wisdom of God, and not in the wisdom of the world. God calls for messengers who will be true reformers. We must educate, educate, to prepare a people who will understand the message and then give the message to the world* (*Testimonies, Series B*, no. 11, page 30).

21 **Q: Is there a time established when Jesus must come?**

A: *Early Writings*, page 75 says: *Time has not been a test since 1844, and it will never again be a test. The Lord has shown me that the message of the third angel must go and be proclaimed to the scattered children of the Lord, but it must not be hung on time.*

22 **Q: Why should we move out to the country now? Why not wait until the Sunday Law is passed?**

A: We should move out now as an indicator of our loyalty and love for Jesus, simply because He has asked us to. It also reveals that we wish to be detached from the world as soon as possible. We cannot afford to postpone any opportunity for spiritual growth.

Send the children to schools located in the city, where every phase of temptation is waiting to attract and demoralize them, and the work of character building is tenfold harder for both parents and children (*Fundamentals of Christian Education*, p. 326).

23 **Q: Are you telling people to "run out!" rather than move to the country in an orderly way?**

A: There will be a time in the last days similar to the experience of the Christians in Jerusalem during AD 70, when we will have to flee (run) in a hurry (Matthew 24:15-22). Now, in this time of probation, we want to follow God's plan as He has counseled; *Those who have felt at last to make a move, let it not be in a rush, in an excitement, or in a rash manner, or in a way that hereafter they will deeply regret that they did move out. . . . Country Living, p. 25:2).* Another implication of this question is that by "running out", we will not be back to minister. This would not be in harmony with God's plan for evangelism as outlined on page 77 of the book *Evangelism* (see also question #8).

24 Q: What is the correct motivation for getting ready for the Lord's coming?

A: 2 Timothy 4:7, 8, *The Desire of Ages*, page 480, and my fond memories of Uncle John.

I have fought a good fight, I have finished [my] course, I have kept the faith: Henceforth there is laid up for me a crown of righteousness, which the Lord, the righteous judge, shall give me at that day: and not to me only, but unto all them also that love his appearing (2 Timothy 4:7-8)

It is not the fear of punishment, or the hope of everlasting reward, that leads the disciples of Christ to follow Him. They behold the Saviour's matchless love, revealed throughout His pilgrimage on earth, from the manger of Bethlehem to Calvary's cross, and the sight of Him attracts, it softens and subdues the soul. Love awakens in the heart of the beholders. They hear His voice, and they follow Him (The Desire of Ages, p.480).

Love is really *the only motivational force* that can get us—and keep us—ready for the arrival of our Best Friend. When I was a young boy, about 9-years-old, we lived in a very run down, abandoned streetcar. We were migrant farm workers. We wanted to get one of the tenement apartments but couldn't afford it. In the winters we were on welfare. My father was extremely dictatorial and abusive, often beating my sister and me with anything he could lay his hands on. I sometimes a thought that I would probably be killed by one of his violent outbursts. Dad often took our welfare check down to the local tavern to gamble it in hopes to increase the amount of money, but most often returned home empty-handed. Hence, the last two weeks of the month we had very little food in the house. I would go to the garbage cans to find pop and beer bottles for resale so that I could buy food for my sister and me.

The bright spot in this situation was my Uncle John. When he would send word that he was coming to visit he would ask if I "had my stuff ready". I knew what he meant. My "stuff" was stored in a tobacco can; twenty feet of fishing line, a well-used hook, and a cork that I had found in a discarded wine bottle. When Uncle John said he would come, I knew he would. Even if he was delayed, my enthusiasm remained high. Why? Because he represented a few hours of liberation from my abusive environment! Nothing could discourage my anticipation of his coming.

So it is in the world today. We can all agree that it is an abusive environment. This world is not our home. We want to be with Jesus, just like I wanted so desperately to be with my Uncle John. My preparations were made because of my love for him, not because someone was forcing me or urging me to be ready. I longed for my Uncle John to come and be with me, just as we want Jesus to be with us. Such motivations as time-setting, dated charts, and conspiracy theories fall far short of God's ideal motivational factor. When we fall in love with Jesus, it will be pure joy to "have our stuff ready"!

Recommended Reading

Education, by Ellen G. White

Country Living, by Ellen G. White

Studies in Christian Education, by E. A. Sutherland

From City to Country Living, by E. A. Sutherland and A. L. White

You Can Survive!, by Jere Franklin

Out of the Cities, by Dave Westbrook

Index